Uneasy Faith

How to Survive Religious Trauma
without Sacrificing Spirituality

Joseph A Onesta

ISBN: 978-1-7361870-3-6

First Printing: January 2021

Integrity HPI

Human Performance Improvement

IntegrityHPI.com

Why Read This Book?

Every person who has suffered religious trauma has a story to tell. Sometimes those stories are hard to hear and even harder to tell. Healing comes both in the telling and the listening. I was a victim of religious trauma and for years I found my story hard to tell because of the emotions that would well up inside me whenever I was unable to avoid thinking about it. Later, perhaps in hindsight, I realized my own strength of character and eventually stopped blaming myself, which also helped me to stop blaming others.

As a Christian and later as an ordained minister, I was both victim and perpetrator of religious trauma. I have caused others to experience feelings of inadequacy, judgment, guilt, and condemnation by the things I said and did, as well as the things I failed to say or do but should have. I never lacked earnest sincerity despite questioning and even doubting.

If you have been hurt, damaged, or abused in a religious context, by a person, a church or a denomination, this book is for you. If you feel uncomfortable with some of the things you see or experience in church or when you encounter religious people, this book is for you. If you are in a position of religious authority, you need to read this book so that you do not inflict religious trauma on others. I can talk about it and present it in this book without reliving any of the emotions that came with the experiences. It is even difficult for me to manufacture emotions over the events that led to my distancing myself from many of the people that I loved.

I believed there was something wrong with me and I expected my relationship with God to heal and restore me. Many expressions of Christianity still believe that homosexuality is a sin that must be corrected for a person to have a proper relationship with God. I have come to understand that my sexuality was and is a natural aspect of my life. It was through coming to love and respect myself as a human being that I began to understand and embrace the life and the love that came naturally to me and in that context, accept the grace that God extends to us all.

Our stories may be different, but we have a shared experience. We have been betrayed by our own belief. Our faith, our church, and often the people we love have not only let us down, but they may also have abandoned us. And while our stories are different, the way to resolve the conflict is nearly the same. Trauma in a religious context can leave deep scars. While many of us are glad to have escaped the context in which the trauma happened, we carry part of that experience with us and many have found themselves suspended in a nowhere land of hurt, anger and bitterness. Uneasy Faith follows my own experience as a victim of religious traumatic experience and provides the key elements of how I not only survived being a victim but became a victor.

Foreword

by C. Roy Hunter, DIMDHA, DAPHP

As of the writing of this Foreword, I just finished reading *Uneasy Faith: How to Survive Religious Trauma without Sacrificing Spirituality* by Joseph A. Onesta. The author of this book relates his personal experiences. The reason this book is personal to me is because I spent 18 year of my life in a religious cult. After leaving, I dealt with religious trauma for almost a decade.

When I was only twelve, my mother became a member of what became known as the Worldwide Church of God. After attending their religious college and earning a bachelor's degree with a major in theology, I worked at their worldwide headquarters for almost eight years.

Like so many religious cults, that organization taught that they were "God's one and only true Church." Unfortunately, the church leaders (or rulers) took unfair advantage of their members to fatten the finances of the Church leaders, and to instill fear into those who would dare to disobey the doctrines of what they called, "God's true Church."

Upon realizing that many of their doctrines were wrong, leaving that church was very traumatic. I had to quit my job at their world headquarters, sell my home, lose my friends because I was "disfellowshipped" (like some people being "excommunicated" or censured from my friends), and move my family to another state in order to start a new life. For several years I went from one church to another, hoping to find a comfortable replacement for my previously misplaced faith.

The religious trauma that I experienced was real enough to give me many nightmares, combined with guilt during the 1970's. I also felt low self-esteem as a result of realizing how gullible I was to ever be devoted to that false church. In addition, I missed many of my former friends who were not allowed to have any contact with me because I was a "lost soul who left the Church."

Unlike the author of this book, I was fortunate to simply become an employee rather than a minister; but that did not prevent me from suffering emotional trauma for years after uprooting my previous life. Over nine years after leaving that cult, I became certified in hypnotherapy; and then realized how religious cults work.

There are five ways to program the subconscious mind: repetition (the slow way), authority (desire to obey or rebel), ego (the desire for identity – be like others or different from others), hypnosis/self-hypnosis, and emotion (the most powerful way to program the subconscious). Religious cults use all five methods of programming your subconscious:

1. Doctrines or dogmas are repeated often.
2. The so-called leaders or ministers are alleged to represent God (and speak with authority).
3. It appeals to our desire to belong to "God's one and only true Church" – and most people have a desire to belong to a group of people they identify with.
4. Sermons are often preceded with prayer and/or meditation, as well as "special music" which literally hypnotizes people into accepting the suggestions of the minister.
5. The sermons are often used to stir up emotions, such as fear of punishment for disobeying God, the "joy" of being "one of God's chosen people" to be saved, etc., etc.

That realization helped me to understand how religious cults can program even well-educated people to become and remain loyal members.

Unlike me, Joseph Onesta was a minister. He shares his personal experiences from his own point of view. His road was different than mine; but like me, he also became certified in hypnotherapy. Whether or not you agree with some of the author's opinions, anyone who escaped a religious cult can learn from the author's experiences in dealing with religious trauma that usually accompanies leaving a religious cult.

As I mentioned earlier in this Foreword, this book was personal to me because of my own success in overcoming religious trauma. It was real; but I am grateful that it is behind me now. My past religious trauma is only a memory of a profound learning experience. I do not choose to give my power away again as I did from age 12 to age 30.

Be wise and learn from the experiences of others so that you may avoid making the same mistakes.

Table of Contents

Chapter 1

Do you have experience

with religious trauma?

"*Do you have experience with religious trauma?*" the voice on the other end of the phone asked. He introduced himself. He was a psychiatrist with a patient that needed a different kind of help. I had heard from other clients that he was "good." Usually, by this, they meant that he listened to them without a prescription pad in his hand.

"Lots," I admitted, "From both sides. I was a victim, and I am sure, as a minister, I have likely caused it in others. I can probably help. What can you tell me about your patient?"

There it was a looming specter of my past. On the day I attempted to resign from the ministry, the senior pastor, in refusing my resignation paraphrased Romans 11:29. "The gifts and callings of God are irrevocable." He said, "You can no more resign than I can accept your resignation. Take all the time you need. Consider it a sabbatical."

1

I set off to get my life in order. I was convinced that staying in a position of spiritual authority was inauthentic while so much of my own life was unsettled, insecure, and unstable. I was not questioning my faith nor my expression of faith. I just did not think I should be in the position of telling people what they should believe when my own experience did not always match what was coming out of my mouth. No matter how much I believed it to be the ultimate truth, it was not manifest in my experience.

I was ordained in the full-gospel or Pentecostal tradition. That tradition is best explained in the simple phrase: *God does not change*. What the apostles experienced, we can experience, including miracles, the gifts of the Spirit, healing, prophecy, and divine intervention at virtually every turn. Everything that happened back then can happen now. I believed in using the word of God, understood the Bible, as a tool, for bringing about those things. If I remained in line with the scriptures, I could expect miracles. If miracles did not manifest, it was that I had lacked faith.

I speak honestly when I say I lacked no faith, and I was convinced that my understanding of the scriptures was good. I had been trained well, in the scriptures and Pentecostal tradition, if not in formal theology, which came into my life much later. I had a gift when I prayed for others, put my hands on the sick, taught the scriptures, preached from the pulpit, taught Sunday School, led Bible Study, or counseled congregants, Miracles do happen. I saw them. And yet, in my own life, I struggled.

Like the apostle Paul, I had a thorn in my side which God had seen fit not to remove, despite all my supplication, my prayer, my self-discipline, my repentance and on several occasions, my formal deliverance. I even repented of the temptation. I knew that being tempted was no sin, but. I still believed that I was somehow failing.

I left the senior pastor's office thinking I would be back soon, that this *sabbatical* was what God wanted, just He and me alone for a time. I had been offered a contract to spend a year in Kuwait. It would be a temporary time off, a true sabbatical for me to get my head straight, seek God, and get in line with the purpose I believed He had for me.

What I did not understand was a lot. I did not realize that all pastors, like all Christians, struggle, perhaps more than others because they are prone to all sorts of temptations that most people do not face. People look up to them, quote them, attribute power to them and many pastors fall prey to the temptation. When they do, the potential for inflicting religious trauma is greatly increased.

I also believed that having sound doctrine would organize and order a person's life in a practical way. I thought that when a person struggled, they were lacking instruction, discipline, or willingness to submit to God's authority. I lacked none of these but still, I struggled. I thought it was my fault. I thought my problems and my struggles were somehow different, more serious, than those of the people I counseled. They were not.

I failed to see that sincere faith and prayer did not guarantee the result I desired. I could not escape the feeling that something was wrong. I had an uneasy faith.

I had suffered a series of traumas from the well-intentioned influence of pastors, elders, evangelists, preachers, and fellow congregants. My own dogmatic approach to a walk of faith had traumatized myself and others.

The senior pastor was right, in a way. I have never stopped being a minister, that is, someone who cares about and for the spiritual wellbeing of others. I did not return to being a pastor. I did visit the church a couple of times after leaving, but I never went back to stay. As it turned out, my time out of the country, resolved a lot of my conflict but not in the way I had expected.

A lot of time has passed since Easter Sunday, 1986, the day I was ordained. I have never been able to completely divorce myself from ministering to the spiritual and emotional needs of others. Although my definitions of those terms and the parameters by which I minister have broadened considerably.

I have to admit, a minister is who I am. I cannot say I *became* a minister on the day that hands were laid on me and I was set apart for service. It was only the day that I formally stepped into a role that had already manifested in my life. I am a minister, not a pastor of a congregation but one who perhaps stands on the fringes of the flock offering gentle guidance and an expression of the love of God which is absolute and unconditional and that I remain.

His patient was in the process of separating from his wife. They had agreed to divorce. The marriage was not working, and no amount of effort could help either of them believe that staying together was a positive thing. They had no children. They both wanted the marriage to end amicably. Neither held grudges. They had consulted a licensed marriage and family therapist (LMFT), who agreed that separation and divorce would be a viable resolution.

Because of the divorce, they were both being shunned by the church where the man had grown up. Their pastor had counseled them that it was God's will for them to remain married and that the wife should submit to her husband's direction.

Neither of them wanted this. Neither of them thought that staying together was anything but financially practical. There were no children involved.

The patient, soon to be my client, was comfortable with the decision to divorce but the divorce meant that he was losing his church. But for a rebellious brother who had left the church as a teen and with whom he had recently been in contact, he was also losing his family. The entire context of his physical, social and emotional life was falling apart.

"It is extreme anxiety. The medications are not really working for him. He's seeing a therapist but there isn't much progress."

I assured the doctor I would welcome his patient. After all, I had been there myself. I promised to keep him informed of our progress and collaborate with his therapist if the client permitted.

He assured me that the therapist would be open to consultation.

I am the survivor of two Christian organizations; one could have been a cult in the making and the other was definitely a religiously abusive cult. The first was a college fellowship. At the time, the fellowship was not a cult but was influenced by charismatic leaders who later went on to form a consortium of churches involved in a practice called shepherding, which established hierarchies of obedience within the members. During my time there, there were only slight hints of shepherding. I have no idea what happened after I graduated.

The second, my first adult church commitment, happened in graduate school. I enthusiastically joined a community church with a very dynamic preacher who seemed to have astonishing revelations about the scriptures. The theological tomes that filled the shelves in his office should have clued me in on the source of his *revelations*, but I believed it was all straight from God. The members said he was *anointed* because of the dynamic nature of his preaching and teaching. We actually brought notebooks to church. I felt like I was privy to a great movement of understanding. Indeed, I learned a lot there. I committed myself to membership which set me a bit apart from other students in the congregation.

After graduation, I tried to stay in the area but the opportunities for gainful employment were not there. I was anxious about leaving but I was engaged to a wonderful woman at the time and believed we would eventually be in the mission field. I needed to earn some money to devest myself of student loans. I took a job teaching at City University of New York, Lehman College in the Bronx.

I had expected and counted on the emotional support of my brothers and sisters in the church. When, after several months, I returned for a visit, my engagement was over and I was shunned, kept at arm's length. There were no smiles, no hugs, and only polite interest in how I was doing. One or two asked if I were coming back and when I said that was impossible, the conversation quickly ended with politeness. I sat alone in a pew, suffering sideways glances and looks of disappointment from people whom I had deeply loved and who I had thought deeply loved me. I walked out of that building feeling more alone in the world than I had ever felt in my life.

When we read about religious trauma, it is almost always in reference to individuals who have separated themselves from a church or religious group. Their trauma is often increased by that separation, though a number of smaller traumas likely led to their leaving. They may have left voluntarily. Or they may have been banned or excommunicated. All of them feel the excruciating pain of isolation and the astonishing revelation that their experience in that group had been somehow less intimate or significant than what they thought it was. For many, it is that revelation that leaves a gaping hole in their heart and their psyche.

In losing their church, they also lose their friends, their families, and often their main reference points in life. They lose their purpose and their safety net. They lose the very context of their lives. They may feel betrayed. They may feel duped. They may feel angry at the church, at the leaders, at members of the congregation, at God and at themselves. In response to their trauma, anger, and bitterness, many become rabid atheists.

Anger, when left untreated, becomes bitterness and bitterness, like a parasite, consumes the human psyche. There is nothing more destructive than bitterness. Ostensibly anger appears as a defense strategy, but when it becomes bitterness, it devours the human spirit from the inside out.

A visit to religious trauma forums reveals some exceptionally angry, bitter people who have abandoned their faith or feel their faith has abandoned them. They rail against the religion, the church and anyone who is stupid enough to believe that stuff. They are left in a state of *not believing*.

The state of not-believing is difficult to navigate. Everyone believes something but the victim of religious trauma who has separated from a group is left only with *not believing*. There is no positive direction in *not* believing. A person who is escaping, only wants to get away but has no plan of where they are to go.

In this way, many victims of religious trauma float in a nowhere land trying to piece together a life in a new context. It is no surprise that they create a community of bitterness in their support groups. At least they have a context. Their ability to trust others has been damaged. They may be alone and lonely. If they tell their story, outsiders do not understand how or why they could have ever believed what they did. They are anxious, fearful, and often exceptionally angry and bitter.

It is a mistake to believe that one event causes dissolution of one's faith. It is, instead. a series of events, overlooked details, excuses made, other things ignored, some large, some small that string together like beads until one day, the string breaks and the beads scatter. The victim flees in fear and confusion no less severe than the people of Pompei as Vesuvius erupted, never to return to the life that they had once known.

This book, *Uneasy Faith*, is about religious trauma but is not only directed at people who have severed their ties and are in the process of creating a new life, but also those who are experiencing those smaller traumas that may lead up to a break. It is my hope that some of my readers can avoid the worst of religious trauma, that they learn to mature gracefully into their own expression of true spirituality, whether that involves leaving their church or existing peacefully with in it. If they choose to exit, they should have a positive direction, one that taps into something essential inside them, their authentic spirituality.

It is sad to me that many of the people who have experienced religious trauma sacrifice spirituality in the process of recovery. That does not need to happen. Spirituality is not dogma, doctrine or even the scriptures. True spirituality is as unique as an individual. It is defined from within.

Sometimes people find spirituality in the context of an existing belief system. They are somehow self-aware enough to understand that where they differ from the teachings of the organization; it is a mere difference. Many Roman Catholics, for example, practice birth control without the slightest misgivings though birth control is prohibited by church doctrine.

I used to be offended when people would say that my expression of the faith was my *interpretation* as if interpretation is somehow wrong or offensive to God. Interpretation is an essential element of our interaction with the Devine.

Spirituality can help define our role and purpose in life. Spirituality is more about living a full life with relative peace and purpose. Spirituality gives a person a sense of belonging to a community and the deeper your spirituality, the bigger that community is. Spirituality is the context in which a human being thrives and grows. Spirituality is that part of every person that comes to understand both their extreme value and their simultaneous insignificance.

Projecting the need for strict adherence to a dogma while simultaneously creating an isolated congregation or even a denomination replete with its jargon, slang, and argot, in my view, is a fundamental failure of the body of Christ. We were not ever meant to be separatists especially from one another.

I have made a couple of large moves in my life, and I have always found it off-putting when visiting a new potential church home that some person from the welcome committee greets me and starts asking questions that seem chatty but serve the purpose of defining what kind of Christian I am. Attend that service a few weeks in a row and eventually get invited to the new member class, which is yet another kind of filter. *If you want to attend our church, you need to know what we believe.* Sounds good, but the subtle message is clearly, "Know what we believe and what you will need to believe as well."

In 324 CE, when Constantine, the emperor of Rome declared Christianity to be the official religion of Rome, there was an immediate jockeying for position. In 325 CE, the first Council of Nicaea was held to determine what form official Christianity would take. Religious leaders gathered to decide what doctrines were correct, and which were not. They examined collections of scriptures and decided which books best fit the emerging power structure. They then canonized those scriptures (declared them inspired by God) while declaring the others, heretical. Some Christians, for lack of political influence, were completely left out of the mix.

That is the story in a nutshell, and it was men being political and wanting their piece of the Roman endorsement that caused brother to revile brother. Even then people believed different things and the winners always say that God was on their side, but the losers believed the same thing and chose to go it alone.

It seems these days that it is increasingly unfashionable to be a Christian but that is hardly persecution. In any case, in western society, much of the anti-Christian sentiment seems well-deserved because the most vocal people who identify as Christian are frankly priggish, lacking in compassion and devoid of even a hint of the love that Jesus expressed as he walked the earth. In precious few of them do we see the humility of the Christ who, at the last supper, stripped to the waist and washed the feet of his disciples, including those of Judas.

The wonderful thing is that we *do* see that love on an individual basis in all sects of Christendom, even in sects that have been labeled as heretical. It seems to me that God's love can transcend doctrinal differences.

Many Christians have somehow forgotten what it means to be *in* this world. They prefer to emphasize not being *of* it. They have voluntarily separated themselves from life on this planet. They fight political battles to defend a gospel that is not good news for anyone, not even them. It is as if for them, the whole purpose of life on earth is to populate their version of heaven.

There are those of us who understand that our eternity has already started. More to the point, God and the gospel does not need anyone to defend them. The gospel is more than John 3:16. It has nothing to do with heaven or hell but the life we live here and now.

A fair number of Christians have absolutely lost their vision and without it, they are perishing. They see the world in such polarized terms that they are incapable of coping with anyone who inhabits the middle ground. For them, faith is not inclusive but exclusive. In or out, turn or burn!

When we see people who are different from us, who do we see? If we consider them as *other*, we dehumanize them. Without realizing it, we sacrifice the very thing we seek to preserve. We have become hypocrites, hiding behind masks, invested in the façade of piety and holiness, but whose secrets reek with mold and decay. Thus, many of us have become like the Sadducees and the Pharisees, white-washed tombs filled with dead men's bones. (Matthew 23:27-28)

If your faith is sometimes a bit uneasy, this book is for you. If your faith is a lot uneasy, this book is for you. If you have already walked away from faith and seek to fill the gaping hole in your spirit, this book is for you. Your personal story may significantly differ from

11

mine, but I hope that my experience will help you better navigate your own.

I have no intention of trying to tell you what you should or should not believe. I will not use the scriptures as a means for proving my point except to draw the reader's attention to certain elements of faith. Instead of the letter of the law, I wish to content myself with what I understand to be the spirit of the law. Therefore, I will paraphrase scriptures when I think it is important to communicate the meaning that I take from them, providing the biblical reference.

Sometimes, I will simply place a biblical reference in parentheses because I think the reader would benefit from reading those verses at in that context. At no place in this book have I directly quoted any verse or particular translation of the scriptures, which as we know, can indicate a doctrinal stance. My hope and intent are that you may consider it valuable to read those scriptures, from whatever translation of the bible you use, when I reference them. Looking them up, however, is up to you.

I have no desire to debate the minutia of verses, or what the words are in Greek, Hebrew, or Aramaic. If you disagree or find my paraphrases offensive, I am sorry. Although my offending some readers is a likely outcome, I do not intend to be offensive. If you are grievously offended, I suggest you read a different book, one that agrees with your theology. I prefer to express in this volume what the scriptures mean to me, especially those parts that helped me confront the most difficult aspects of my religious trauma. If they help you, great. If you fling this book into the bonfire, have at it.

Chapter 2

Religious Traumas, Plural

If you do an internet search on religious trauma, you will find a veritable barrage of material focusing on people who reckon they have been duped into some belief system. Many of them report having been emotionally bullied and some, sexually or physically abused. Often, they present their former church, group, or organization as a cult from which they were glad to escape.

If we are honest about it, most faith-based groups are inherently involved in some sort of manipulative behaviors and mindsets. The very idea of the group is a sense of conformity to a standard or norm. Sometimes the manipulation is gentle; other times, it can be exceptionally severe. Conformity to a community norm is a choice with consequences.

However, being bullied, psychologically, emotionally, or even physically into conformity is the practice of a cult. When sanctions are applied to individuals who do not quite fit the mold to which members are to conform, even gentle manipulation becomes extortion. And, as in the case of a confession extracted under torture, the sincerity or truthfulness of the confession, or in this case, the declaration of faith, is suspect.

Whether the organization qualifies as a cult or not, we need to understand that social pressure to conform goes well beyond the auspices of a religious organization. All social environments establish norms and mores based on shared values. Ostensibly in the United States, we value individualism, yet most people seek others who think or act as they do. And members of many groups, either consciously or unconsciously, establish boundaries between themselves and those who are noticeably different.

The social fear of being labeled as different causes a fair number of people to falsely present themselves as being like the others, effectively wearing a mask to fit in. When a group labels the difference as sinful, the stakes are raised to an unfortunate level.

In 1986 I was ordained through the laying on of hands in church in the Bronx, New York. The organization called itself interdenominational, but it was mostly Pentecostal. The senior pastors were ordained Foursquare ministers. Foursquare, a denomination in its own right, was originally organized around the radio ministry of Aimee Semple McPherson. At the time of my ordination, I believe the denomination was under the leadership of Jack Hayford. I had no direct association with Foursquare denomination. I provide this information for those who want to know what my doctrinal stance was at the time. I was conservative, well-versed but quite literal in my use of the Bible, and enthusiastic for the kingdom of God.

That was quite some time ago. Since that date, I have been through a spiritual wringer. I know others who have left the church because of the religious trauma they suffered. They have denounced their faith because of the manipulation of the church and the consequences of their not fitting the established mold.

I was fortunate that in my own struggle and need to be what we called "right with God," I found my own authenticity without sacrificing my spirituality. I admit I eventually lost many of the polarizing, in or out, turn or burn ideologies that were part of my life at the time. The process was painful but liberating. Although I was hurt, and sometimes angry, I did not become bitter nor resentful. Today, I experience a more sincere faith and a deeper, more reliable relationship with the divine.

My own experience is Christian, but much of what I describe in this book is not unique to Christianity. I have worked with people from a broad array of faiths and have seen similar struggles among them all. It speaks to me of a kind of universal spiritual need that religion is intended to fill, but occasionally fails to do so.

Russell Brand, a British actor, and self-styled philosopher, describes spirituality as a combination of awareness, purpose, and direction. I can appreciate the simplicity of that definition in stark contrast to the common Christian need to be correct in theology, adherent to dogma and doctrine, and socially acceptable within the church community.

Religious trauma does not come solely from the malfeasance of cult leaders seeking power, control, and money. It happens as a result of very well-meaning people seeking to establish a spiritual calm in their lives, a place where they can be fully comfortable, even if it means denying others the same benefit. Traumas can come from a biting remark "said in love." They come from phrases like, "Love the sinner: hate the sin." They come from cold shoulders, gossip, people

15

jockeying for position in church politics and from a lack of appreciation for volunteer labor that often goes above and beyond the norm.

We perpetrate religious trauma on one another, most often unwittingly, but sometimes consciously, thinking we are making a point. Like a compulsive gambler at a slot machine, we have already invested too much to walk away from even petty confrontations. We keep going yet a while longer, waiting for the payout but all the while digging a deeper and deeper hole.

Religious trauma comes in many forms. Consider the disappointment of a congregation when the human frailty of a pastor is exposed. Think of the disappointment of earnestly praying for something only to see manifest the opposite of one's intentions. Asking for a miracle, believing it will be, but it does not happen. We might be confused by the atrocities we see in the world or the hate and divisiveness in the church. We may have been mistreated by people who publicly declare their faith while privately behaving in despicable, cruel ways.

If you find yourself experiencing a kind of disillusionment, a conflict between what you see in the church and what you have been told the church is or should be, welcome to the party. This book is for you and may well be about people like you.

In this book, I am going to transparently share my own journey and recount some of the conflicts I have witnessed in friends and clients who have sought my help coping with trauma experienced at the instigation of religious people and organizations, even entire established denominations.

My journey may parallel or significantly differ from your own but rest assured, we are both headed toward the same objective, living an authentic life that includes our essential need for spirituality, or as Russell Brand suggests, our need for awareness, purpose, and direction.

At one point in my life, I would have sought to persuade you to believe like me. Let me assure you again, that I have no intention of telling you what you should or should not believe. I hope, however, you dig deep, find even the tiniest kernel of your own belief, nurture it and let it grow and mature. If you do, it will be like a mustard seed, which starts out small and ends up a rather impressive plant.

Let me illustrate. I keep a vegetable garden. From season to season, I will plant different crops in the same bed. Sometimes a self-seeded volunteer plant from the prior season pops up. Whenever possible, I like to leave them instead of plucking them out like a weed. Whenever I have chosen to let volunteer plants grow, they usually produced remarkable harvests. That kind of robust seed of faith is precisely what we are looking for.

As you read through this work, try not to judge me. I am here to help you but my only way of doing that is relating to you as a fellow human, a fellow struggler. We may not have had the same struggles but we both have struggled.

Whenever I find myself discussing the challenges of spiritual life, especially with strong-minded Christians who refuse to listen to anything that does not already agree with their views, I find myself smiling and saying with the greatest intention of love, "You know. The only real difference between us is that you think you are correct, and I know that in some way, both of us are wrong." They rarely react to that statement. I wonder if they even understand it or if they just think I am admitting my own fallibility in deference to them.

You may have heard a phrase like, we cannot compare apples to oranges. A big part of our problem comes from starting off with a bunch of different seeds of faith and trying to only grow one kind of fruit. If you start off with an apple seed and I start off with an orange, no matter how hard we try, neither of us will ever produce a pear. And if we let that fact frustrate us, we have wasted a lot of time, effort, and potential when we could have had a great harvest of apples and oranges.

It is important to understand that we are believing creatures. Faith and belief are essential to our survival, even in a merely physical sense. We know this through science. The central function of memory is to allow us to effectively predict day-to-day outcomes. If our ability to trust our own perceptions is undermined, we become helpless.

Many of the victims of severe religious trauma gave up trusting their own perceptions. They allowed some preacher, deacon, leader, teacher, guru, denomination, religion, or philosophy to think for them. They somehow grew to believe that questioning was synonymous with doubting. They decided to blindly trust those further along in the game and when their trust was proven baseless, their lives were seemingly destroyed.

If you join me on this journey, I ask only one thing. Please think for yourself. I admit that during my own journey, virtually all of my dogmas and doctrines were stripped away until all I had left was the kernel, the very seed I started out with and was finally in a position to nurture it and see what it would become, rather than trying to force to be like someone else's tree. It was not a pleasant journey, but I am truly glad to have travelled it.

Chapter 3

The Final Sermon

I had already decided that I would be temporarily stepping away from the ministry. Everything was all but decided. I had the offer to go to Kuwait as a safety net and it seemed that God was putting things in order so that I would get my time alone with Him. Even then, I felt as if I were being led out into the desert to be tempted. While much of Kuwait actually is desert, the desert I perceived was being a Christian in a Muslim country. It would be just me and God and together we could confront and conquer that part of my life that had become inflamed, swollen, and painful. Like a splinter that becomes infected, I needed to pull that thorn out of my side.

I was not afraid of going to a Muslim country. I had been teaching English as a Second Language for years and knew students from all over the world. Indeed, I had been invited to Kuwait by a student whose brother wanted me to work with corporate executives on their English and cross-cultural skills.

Muhammad was my student in a Monday, Wednesday and Friday class that met at noon. Muslims pray at noon especially on

Fridays and Muhammad asked me if he could miss class every Friday to attend services at the Mosque. As we sat in my office, I calculated the best possible grade for class participation he could get if he were to miss thirty percent of the classes. He was disappointed.

"Teacher, it is my religion."

I said, "Well, why did you register for this course knowing it would conflict with your attending the Mosque?"

"It was the only class open," he replied.

Remember, I was a pastor. It was hard to pull the wool over my eyes. I could see my student's struggle, his confusion, and his sincere desire to do what was right. I answered, "Ok now, go to the mullah and ask for his wisdom. What would Allah want you to do? Would Allah want you to sacrifice your grade so you could pray at noon on Friday for fifteen weeks or should you honor God by being a good student, getting a good grade and praying before or after class?"

His eyes widened and a smile broadened his face. "Teacher, you are a Muslim!"

"Not with a capital M," I answered. Islam is easily translated as *submission to God*. A *muslim* using a small *m* might mean one who is submitted to God, a person of the book, in other words, a Christian or a Jew. Not many people realize that Jews, Muslims, and Christians actually share the same God. I continued, "Many of us have to make decisions like this, even Christians."

Muhammad never missed class after that, and early the following semester, he extended the invitation to spend a year or two in Kuwait helping the executives in his brother's company internationalize. As I was already considering stepping away from the ministry to get my head on straight, I accepted the offer and began studying Arabic.

I was asked to preach the Sunday before I was to meet with the senior pastor. There are many denominations that use a thing called the *lectionary*. A lectionary is a volume that divides the Bible into a three-year schedule of verses meant to be topical for sermons. In those denominations, a person could attend any church in the denomination on any given day and hear a sermon prepared on a specific set of scriptures. In some ways the lectionary is a beautiful expression of unity.

In the Pentecostal tradition, we do not follow a lectionary. Preachers certainly do build up a stock of sermons, but instead of following the lead of a schedule, we take prayerful time to seek God for the message we should deliver to the congregation. If I am totally honest about it, sometimes we wing it, relying on the Holy Spirit to take over at the last minute. I wondered what I would ever do if I had nothing; if as I stood up to preach, there would be no inspiration what-so-ever. It never happened, but I imagined standing up in front of the congregation and simply saying, "I got nothing. Let's just worship."

I spent time in the scriptures, praying, and asking God for the message he would have me deliver. What did the congregation need to hear? I found the gospels to always be a good place to start. I was reading about the man who asked Jesus what the greatest commandment was. I will paraphrase Jesus' response. *Love God with your entire being. But Jesus did not stop there. Love each other as you love yourselves* (Matthew 22:34-40). I contemplated that passage, wondering how much I actually loved myself. I had been waiting for God to fix a persistent problem in my life, a nearly constant temptation. In a way, I believed that if the problem were gone, I would be more acceptable to God. I realized that being acceptable to God was not the core issue. I was not acceptable to myself. I had been postponing self-love until I became a better person.

From my experience in pastoral counseling, I knew this sentiment to be common. We all want to do better, to be better, and I saw that desire as a trait of a genuine, contrite heart. But I also had encountered a double-standard. There were certain people whose struggles centered around things that made them appear less than others. Let's face it, in the Christian world, whether we like to admit it or not, some behaviors or attitudes which are seen as sins are less offensive than others. We can tolerate and easily forgive the sins of a friendly, attractive person but discovering some truly distasteful revelation about a person we dislike produces a degree of intolerance and even condemnation.

I am being intentionally vague here because I do not know you, and because the exact point I am making does not depend on lurid details. But as an example, I provide for you the story of two people whose names in real life actually rhymed.

When I first moved to New York, I stayed with friends and shared a room with another guest of theirs, who was also an ordained minister. One night, I had a very sexual dream, which might well have produced a nocturnal emission. Just before the critical moment, I woke up to find the other guest hovering above me. He muttered something about praying for me as I was having a nightmare. I sleepily took him at his word, but later, I realized that praying was not what he was doing. The thought of what he was actually doing is despicable but not because of his same-sex attraction, which is the aspect most people would focus on. It was despicable because he was taking advantage of me and deriving some form of pleasure out of touching me while I slept. But for many in the Christian world, the more detestable element of this event would be his homosexuality, which is irrelevant to the abuse.

In church, there was another man, who attended with a woman I assumed to be his wife and their little girl. He sometimes led worship, shared his feelings about the scriptures and his love for God. He was an amiable fellow, broadly respected and liked in the congregation. Gossip though it may have been, I later learned that the woman with whom he attended church and with whom he fathered his ill-behaved little girl was not his wife. His wife, who was still his wife, lived elsewhere and attended another church.

The point I am making is that somehow socially accepted behaviors that could be biblically defined as sinful are overlooked while other things, like same-sex attraction, cast long shadows to the point that people impose sanctions against gay people even while apparently discounting other actions that are clearly abusive. That man hovering above me was committing an act of sexual abuse, gay or straight, it was sexual abuse! Somehow that is to be considered no worse than a homosexual who otherwise has exemplary behavior.

Anyone in the position of having to navigate a religious environment that seems inconsistent has to cope with this sort of confusion, and the confusion produces a kind of insecurity that causes people to hide their real issues from one another, saving them for private counseling with the pastor, if they dare mention it at all to anyone.

Let's get back to the sermon. At the time, one of my favorite books in the Bible was 1 John. I clung tenaciously to 1 John 1:9, confessing my sin (it was really just temptation then) and believing that God would not only forgive me but cleanse me of it. The forgiveness I could easily receive, but that cleansing was a long time in coming.

At that time, however, another verse caught my eye. I had read the verse many times, but this time it veritably glowed on the page. Just the sort of thing a full-gospel minister hopes for. I will paraphrase it for you:

People who claim to love God but do not love their fellows, are lying, not only to one another but to themselves and God. (1 John 4:20)

It took me a while to process it and if you have already got the message, I commend you.

Question: How does one demonstrate a love for God?

Answer: By loving other people. It is not by having the right doctrine, being scriptural or biblical or even pious. It is by loving one another.

Question: How should one love other people?

Answer: As one loves oneself.

I had never seen it before. I had assumed that love meant doling out the truth, using the scriptures, and setting behavioral standards. After all, Christian love had to be tough love sometimes. That tough love idea had been instilled in me back in my college days when I was held accountable to older brothers in the Lord who, I understand now, were nothing more than children themselves.

To ultimately express love for God, we have to articulate love and real love for each other. We need to love each other as we love ourselves. If we do not love ourselves, we are therefore incapable of loving each other. And, if we do not love one another, our declaration of our love for God is a lie. I urged the congregation to seek the love that God had for them, to take that standard and apply it first to themselves and then to one another.

I dare say the message fell on deaf ears. In a church where people think that speaking in tongues is a sign of spirituality, where dancing, singing, and raising hands in worship is a sign of the Holy Spirit in you, what more is needed to demonstrate our love for God?

This was the last sermon I delivered as an assistant pastor at the church in the Bronx. I left the congregation that day having explored this message in my heart, and I knew that it had to be love that directed my resignation. One of my biggest challenges over the next year while sojourning in the desert of Kuwait would be to find somewhere under all my emotional baggage, an essential love for myself so that I could genuinely love others and thus express love for God.

Joseph A. Onesta

Chapter 4

A Child of Destiny

E ven if you were raised in a church, there came a day when you were expected to make an adult commitment to your faith. I was raised Roman Catholic and that day for Roman Catholics is called *confirmation.* Confirmation is meant to be a Catholic's day of Pentecost. I remember being terrified that I might speak in tongues when the Bishop slapped me. But I have to admit that I was not a typical Catholic kid, despite being an altar boy, attending twelve years of Catholic Sunday School and becoming a certified CCD teacher.

I spent early Sunday mornings watching Katheryn Kuhlman, perched on a tall stool, wearing an evening, gown, hand elegantly held high declaring, "I believe in miracles." Her weekly show recounted stories of the miracles people experienced attending her meetings. After that or before, I do not remember, was Earnest Angley in his pastel-colored tuxedos, performing miracles on stage. "Say, baby!" He would shout at a presumably deaf person. "BABA" was the response to the cheers of the audience. Oh, yes, and perhaps the most formative in my life was *Davey and Goliath,* a clay-animated children's television series about a boy and his dog facing normal kid challenges and making better Christian choices.

When I went to college, I made another kind of commitment when I responded to an altar call when an evangelist named Larry Tomczak came to campus. Tomczak preached a total commitment to the Lord, and I was taken by that message. I felt that the lack of commitment was what my life had been missing and that Jesus, rather than me, should be the center of my life. I committed myself to Jesus and to that purpose and goal.

After the evangelistic event, I went home and smashed all my albums because committed Christians listened only to Christian music. I also quit smoking cold turkey, something I considered a miracle at the time. I was baptized in the Spirit with the evidence of speaking in tongues. (There, I have just lost half my audience.) I began attending a campus ministry associated with Tomczak. We sang a chorus that I think we learned from him; I don't really know. It started, "I am a child of destiny."

That is how I felt at the time. I was a child of destiny; I was called, and I answered the call. It informed virtually every aspect of my life after that.

Tomczak along with the seminary-trained leader of that campus ministry, Brent Detweiler, went on to be involved in the establishment of Sovereign Grace Ministries with C.J. Mahaney. I name these people only because their involvement in Sovereign Grace Ministries is documented and acknowledged. And the experiences I had with these two leaders are factual.

During my time in the campus fellowship, we practiced a kind of discipleship shepherding, which in some cases grew out of hand. The fellowship ostensibly was an outreach of the Assembly of God Church (AG), but there was not much connection to that denomination when I attended. The students who trekked across town to the Assembly of God church on Sundays were few. I went once but found another church that I preferred. And I remember thinking about the apparent lack of interest the local AG church seemed to have for the campus fellowship, though, in honesty, they may have been the ones to pay for the leadership.

Shepherding is a process of discipleship in which older, more experienced, and presumably more knowledgeable individuals oversee and guide the spiritual practice and development of less experienced or less knowledgeable people. We *lessers* experienced social pressure to conform and in some cases, obey.

Admittedly, this is not vastly different from what took place in the first three hundred years of Christianity, which even then resulted in different schools of thought and practice. The practice of shepherding, however, implies a kind of hierarchy that can leave the group open and vulnerable to opportunistic, clever-minded, manipulative people who have the charisma to rise in the ranks and wield cult-like control over the lives of others.

We were taught to never forget that the words *disciple* and *discipline* share a common root. I rarely encountered the *discipline* of discipleship. One example is worth recounting.

I lived in a house with seven other young men of the fellowship. We rose around 5:00 a.m. to pray and worship, then we would eat a light breakfast, and everyone was off to class which for some, began at 8:00 a.m. Others may well have gone back to bed. We also ate dinner together. I found communal living, for the most part, quite nice and comfortable.

Through much of my university experience, I worked in one of the campus cafeterias. I might have earned a bit more money working somewhere else but working in the cafeteria had the advantage of eating for free. One semester, I shared a nearly identical work schedule with a guy named Liam.

Liam was a small, wiry guy with curly hair that resisted his attempts at spiking it. He did not much like our job at the cafeteria, and he had the occasional air of someone "paying his dues." One thing that greatly animated Liam was punk rock. He played and sang in a band.

After our shift, Liam and I would sit companionably together, eating a meal. He would tell me about his band and how he had been inspired by Sid Vicious and the Sex Pistols. I would tell Liam how I had been inspired by Jesus.

Of course, I hoped that Liam would also be inspired by Jesus, but beyond that, I honestly liked him. We got along very well and if circumstances had been different, I think we might have become great friends. By circumstances, I mean, if I had been permitted to socialize with him more, but I discovered that such a friendship would be impossible unless he joined my ranks and abandoned his own.

Liam constantly invited me to hear his band play in one of the local bars in our college town. This, for a guy who broke all his secular records, created a slight conflict. I honestly was not really interested in bars or punk rock music, but I was genuinely interested in Liam as a friend. Late in that fall semester, Liam was insistent about a gig his band was playing at a bar. It was to be their last gig for the semester, and I *had* to come.

The date coincided with an open house that we were hosting where I lived. I used the open house as an excuse to put Liam off yet one more time. I could see it disappointed him. I had the sense that it hurt him.

Thinking about Liam, I briefly left the open-house event. I was gone for less than an hour. I ran up to the bar where the band was playing. I could hear the music from outside. I slipped into the bar, situated myself up front where the band was playing. They were surprisingly good, and Liam had a decent voice. Though secular music was no longer an interest, I could appreciate his talent and skill.

In a few moments, our eyes met. He saw me, nodded, and smiled. I gave him a thumbs up and slipped out of the bar and went back to the open house.

I can only guess at what clued my housemates as to what I had done during my brief absence from our party. Perhaps I smelled of smoke. Maybe someone saw me enter or leave the bar. Anyone who saw me in the bar would know I never touched a glass to avoid even the appearance of drinking. Perhaps someone followed me. I have no idea, but they knew I had gone into a bar.

The next morning, when I came downstairs to worship, I was greeted by seven stern faces lined up on one side of the room, and I was invited to sit on the other.

I was asked for an explanation of my behavior. I told them about working with Liam, how I had been witnessing to him, how it was his last gig, and I recounted every aspect of what I had done.

However, the request for my explanation was merely perfunctory as no one listened to my response.

The instruction and discipline, however, were clear. I had to give up going to bars or I would be out of the house. Going to bars was never a problem for me and giving them up cost me nothing. I did not bother trying to bring up Jesus hanging out with the tax collectors. But I keenly felt my integrity was unfairly questioned and challenged.

Though I would not have admitted it at the time, witnessing was not the only reason I befriended Liam. I genuinely liked the guy as a human being. We connected, even though our experiences and ideas were vastly different. Like I said before, I think Liam and I might have become good friends if I had not sat opposite the judgment committee that morning. Like my cigarettes and my albums, Liam was gone.

The subtle message of this event was that there was no room for the parts of my life that did not perfectly conform to the community we had formed. I hope you caught the symbolic positioning of the judgment committee lined up on one side of the room and me placed on the other because I was the one who apparently broke rank. It was a hint of the sting to come if I did not toe the line.

There were two messages that day. One was delivered to me. *Conform or you are out.* But that same message was more subtly communicated to everyone in the room, *See what happens to people who break rank.* Years later, one of the brothers from the house tried to make amends letting me know that he came to understand my position, but it was uttered in such hushed tones, at a reunion of the fellowship, that I wondered why his acknowledgement had to remain between us and not out in the open.

I am not suggesting the fellowship was a cult, but I have no difficulty suggesting that if it were not for the transient nature of college students, it could have become one. It was not a socially healthy community. I loved living in community but was left uneasy by the lack of personal expression outside what we all tacitly agreed was the norm.

A healthy community embraces the members and tries to understand and encourage them for their own good and the good of the community. A healthy community listens and considers carefully before passing judgment or authorizing sanctions. A genuinely healthy community finds expulsion of the aberrant person an odious and distasteful last resort.

During the early days of the COVID-19 pandemic in 2020, there were news stories about the response of some churches to the lockdown orders. In the name of freedom of religion, some churches defied the lockdown orders and remained open. Incredulously, I watched news interviews of congregants defiantly not wearing masks as they approached the entrance to the church building, proclaiming that God's grace would protect them from the virus. Today, we may all know what a "spreader event" is because many people who defied those lockdown orders got sick and some, including pastors, died.

Many other pastors opted to serve their congregations by conducting services online via livestream or recorded services. Some congregations conducted Sunday school, home group bible studies and prayer groups via online conference programs.

As I watched the news clips of people walking into church declaring their faith absurdly into the microphones of the reporters, I wondered how many of them were lying. How many were secretly afraid to attend services but felt compelled to do so lest they demonstrate non-conformity, often considered a lack of faith?

I privately celebrated the few who chose to follow the advice of experts and stay home though I mourned the social sanctions that might be applied to them. No doubt that at least some of them began church shopping and others may have stopped attending services entirely.

The fourteenth chapter of the book of Romans teaches us the value of diversity in the Body of Christ. When church communities fail to appreciate this exhortation, they create an environment conducive to and tolerant of cult-like abuse.

I have come to understand that the real Christian community is not found within the walls of a church or under the banner of a denomination, but rather the Body of Christ, **is** the people with all their differences, with all their weaknesses, and with all their unique expression of spirituality. We need not judge one another.

I conformed for my own reasons but in response to social pressure. I quit smoking. I broke my records. I severed old ties. I forfeited opportunities and perhaps sacrificed what might have been a valuable life-long friendship. I entertain no thoughts that any of these sacrifices impressed God at all. They were my choice and, perhaps, my loss.

Chapter 5

A Sincere Faith

I have often wondered about the hundreds of people who go forward to give their lives to Jesus at evangelistic events. Had they been touched by the Holy Spirit or had a fair number of them walked forward out of the simple fear of hell and an internal acknowledgement that they were not as perfect as they would like to be?

I have also wondered how many of them expected Holy Spirit magic in their lives to fix whatever they thought was wrong. That is the sort of thing we hear in testimonies in which people recount all the ways in which they had gone wrong only to end their story with some pat phrase like, ". . .and then I asked Jesus into my heart." They say little or nothing about the struggle after their moment of conversion. They do not expound on their failed attempts to correct behaviors they understand as wrong. They never mention the humiliating sense of not measuring up to the expectations of other Christians. They somehow forget the condescending glances at their brand-new bibles, or the offers to help them find referenced bible verses.

35

Given the sheer numbers who respond to altar calls multiple times, I wonder how many of them are secretly hoping it will somehow be more effective on subsequent trips forward.

Evangelistic tools, events, tracts, books, and movies often emphasize the need to be "right with God," pointing out that all one's problems are a function of not being right with God and the eternal consequences of that condition.

Sometimes I think Christians give the notion of sin all too much press when faith, honest, simple faith should take center stage. In western expressions of Christianity, despite our ability to quote scriptures about grace and faith, we have been trained to believe that our behavior, attitudes, and the doctrines we hold dear have value at the end of our earthly lives. We become convinced that we need not only to be right with God but right about our doctrines and beliefs.

After all, what does "right with God" actually mean? How do we know if we are or are not right with God? That mindset is manipulative and extortionist. In some Pentecostal churches, women who wear makeup or do not wear a head covering are not right with God. A young Pentecostal once rebuked me because I was talking to someone on the subway about Jesus while I had the audacity to wear tennis shorts on a hot and humid day.

I ask sincerely, would you still believe all that you profess to believe even if eternal reward or eternal punishment were removed from the equation?

If we remove the threat of eternal punishment or the fear of the loss of eternal reward, we can be more honest about our expression of faith. In that honesty lies our ability to grow and mature spiritually. Somehow, we have stopped believing the good news and have embraced only the fear of bad news and I contend that we were never ever meant to live in fear.

Emotionally, fear can be crippling and even detrimental to our health. Psychologically fear is used to manipulate and control people into acting contrary to their own core values. Fear can negatively impact our health, make us miserable, and leave us vulnerable to those who would abuse our weakness.

I had struggled with quite a number of aspects of being an assistant pastor. The church was ethnically Puerto Rican and whether in affection or slight derision, being called "el blanquito" (the little white guy) bothered me. The older members who had come from Puerto Rico basically ignored me. It was not the language. I am bilingual.

Indeed, I was the one given the duty to interpret the preaching, delivered almost exclusively in Spanish, into English for the kids in the congregation. The young people liked and respected me. They frequently came to me with their problems and confessions. The most difficult but later liberating thing for me was discovering that I did not have all the answers.

On a particular day, one young man came to me telling me of his experience at what I think was a transcendental meditation retreat. He recounted the meditation experience of leaving his body and it had confused him. He wanted to know what he should believe.

Until my ordination, I had been fully able to tell people what I thought they should believe. But since, the gravity of the advice gave me pause. My own struggles just made me question whether accepting ordination had been wise. I had seen and experienced so much inconsistency and even hypocrisy in the church that it felt like there was much to do but questioned if I were the one to do it.

I remained silently alarmed as he told me about his experience. I wanted to help him. I felt real love and care for the people in my charge, but I no longer knew what to say. I was growing in the idea of sincere faith. Sincere faith meant to me that I should believe something, not merely because the Bible, the pastor or some preacher said so but because I held an inner conviction of the truth. The evidence of that conviction had to be expressed and validated in my life.

In response to the young man's inquiry, I finally uttered perhaps the most spiritually mature statement I had ever made up until that point. "I can tell you what the Bible says. I can tell you what I believe. I can tell you what most people in this church and the other pastors would say. But as for what you really believe, that is for you to tell me." I had no idea that within weeks, I would confront myself with the same challenge.

About that time, a good friend invited me to join him for a two-week visit to California. We would stay with his brother and his brother's partner in Venice Beach. He felt obliged to tell me that the partner was also a man, but they were nice and respectful and would honor my faith. I accepted the offer mostly to get away and to visit Los Angeles.

The two weeks were lovely. We did some touristy things, but mostly I was content to walk along the beach most days, just drinking in the sun and the warmth, stopping for lunch or having an ice-cream. There I could wear shorts with impunity.

The decisive moment in my own crisis of faith happened one evening just before we were to return to New York. My friend wanted to spend the evening alone with his brother. Dillon, the partner, and I were left to our own devices. He enthusiastically invited me to his favorite pizza place.

We walked there. The weather was glorious, a warm breeze off the ocean, and Dillon had a real gift for chatting and leading a conversation. It was nice not to have to think too deeply. I was not his pastor and after all, I was on vacation. The pizza place was distinctly Californian. There were no token pictures of Rome or pastoral scenes of the Tuscan countryside. It was sleek and modern and stylish.

"I like this place a lot," Dillon said. "The pizza is good but even more than that, I like to support local businesses, especially when they openly identify as gay-owned and operated."

I had not noticed the sign nor understood the rainbow flag. In my strictest days, I might have objected but he had been a delightful, welcoming host. The opinion was fair enough, I thought. After all, it was important to him. On the practical side of things, if the pizza had been bad, I would not be buying another slice. It was delicious.

"I admire people who come out of the closet and accept themselves for who they are rather than pretending," Dillon rambled. "Every gay person should do that, don't you think? I do. I think coming out of the closet lets a person live sincerely. It has for me. I love Michael but when push comes to shove, I am the only person I have to live with for the rest of my life. I might as well like me. And you know, I think it goes a long way toward making the world a better place for all gay people. Everyone should come out." He said all this decisively, then added, "When do you think you will?"

I choked. Dillon said no more about it. He remained as social and companionable as always.

That was perhaps the first time in my adult life that I had been outed, even in a private way. I had confessed same-sex attraction to a few people in my college fellowship. That had not gone over well and resulted in my being kept at arm's length by quite a few members. I have no doubt that the word of my confession traveled because other people who experienced same-sex attraction spoke with me in confidence.

So now you know the thorn that was in my side. I cannot tell you how my sexual orientation plagued me. With every Christian milestone, I hoped, I prayed that it would just go away. Up until that point, I had experienced sex only once in my life, and it was unpleasant. I had known other gay people, but given my experience in college, I was not about to talk about it again with anyone.

I do not remember what I said to Dillon if I said anything at all. I recollect my sense of vulnerability as if I had been caught outside in my underwear. I spent the rest of the evening and much of the night reliving the question, unable to put it out of my mind. I did not know what it meant to be gay except for the people who were taunted, even abused for it. Throughout my life, I had been branded a sissy because I just was not like other boys. I was not as aggressive, nor sports minded as most or as boorish as some. I could not even fake it. Once I opened my mouth or moved, the game was up. I was a bit feminine in my mannerisms and my voice inflection. I had paid a high price in bullying, taunting, and rejection but had convinced most people that I was an innocent victim.

Late that night, I arose from my sleepless bed and went out into the quiet courtyard. We were perhaps half a mile from the beach. I am not sure that I could actually hear the waves, or it was just my imagination. Was Dillon just guessing the way the bullies had? Why hadn't I denied it like I always had? Apart from the Christians I knew who were battling the same problem, I had never met regular gay people before. Until I met Michael and Dillon, every gay person I knew had been a stereotype or someone trying to pray it away.

I found myself debating the potential of my being gay with God. You see, up until that moment I had honestly believed that God would take my same-sex attraction away. For the first time, I was asking myself to consider the possibility that God might never take it away.

It started out as a game of *what if* . . . What if I married a woman? What if I chose celibacy for the rest of my life? What if I gave into the lusts of the flesh and ended up lost? What if I had sex with a woman? Would that change me? Why was I this way?

I prayed out loud in the conversational way I felt most comfortable. *I know I've been sincere with you. I have given you everything I have. I know it's not much, but I have given you my life and my sexuality. Your word says that if I believe in you, I am going to heaven at the end of my life. On the other hand, I have always had this attraction for men and according to the bible, that dooms me to hell. I cannot really reconcile these two things. If I am missing something . . . I must be missing something; please help me. I want to be right with you more than anything else. I have not been a hypocrite in my faith, and yet, this thing still plagues me. I have confessed this sin and your word promises that you are faithful and just to cleanse me from all unrighteousness, yet here I stand. Where is the cleansing, the purification your word promises?*

If being attracted to men dooms me to hell, I have been so doomed all my life, and there is nothing to be done about that, at least on my part. I have been conducting my life as faithfully as I know how, seeking your face, your will, confessing my sin and waiting for your faithful cleansing. I have dedicated my life to you, all of it, including my sex drive. There is nothing that I can do to add to the work of the cross. Neither, from what I can see, is there anything more I can do to effect this change. As it is, it feels like I am living a lie.

For the first time in my Christian experience, I felt as if living in the faithful promises of God was an expression of hypocrisy. That very night, transparency began to inch its way into my life. I did not know what decisions I might make in the future. I did not know what would happen. I just knew that heaven and hell had to be removed from the equation. What did I genuinely believe?

I will not divulge the kernel of faith that I salvaged from the wreckage of my life. That is between God and me. If you are experiencing challenges to your faith, it is up to you to discover your own kernel, that tiny seed of faith that remains.

That did not mean I was free from any consequences of my future decisions and I no longer knew what I would decide. Those decisions, however, would bear their consequences in this life and not the next. You might say, in terms of eternity, I had nothing to lose. I was suspended between two truths and in my mind, neither of them could be denied though each excluded the other.

I was not yet ready to declare my life gay-owned and operated. The first time I uttered the words, *I am gay*, they were uttered in a resignation so profound that I wept bitterly for hours. The gay-owned and operated life took nearly another two years. Dillon lived just long enough to see it.

I was ready to think beyond the boundaries of the doctrines that I had accepted so unquestioningly. I still hoped and believed that God would somehow reveal in me latent heterosexual tendencies. However, I gave up my disappointment when the miracle did not come, and later, I no longer looked for it at all.

That very night, something else happened. God began to grow. Well, at least my perceptions of God began to broaden. My prayer life was enhanced because instead of spending my prayer time telling God what was wrong with me, I was able to just be comfortable. I began to learn what it was like to just be with God. I was able to worship and speak my feelings and, yes, even my failings, whatever they might be, without waiting for anything or even thinking that God was waiting for me to do something. I still averted my eyes when I noticed an attractive man. The gesture was an act of respect for him as he was unlikely to feel flattered by my admiration. But I did not look away out of my fear of God's wrath or punishment.

Living in faith does not mean living a lie until it comes true.

My question to you about removing heaven and hell from the equation is relevant. I could not at the time reconcile my sublimated sexuality with the standards of the faith I had been taught. The two did not meet outside of me, but there I was, stuck in the middle with no way to explain or justify what was unavoidably true.

Once heaven and hell were no longer primary concerns for me, I was able to meet my God without fear. After all, who was I trying to kid? I had a lot to work through.

It is not my job to tell you what to believe but rather foster an environment for you to discover, even in tiny increments, what you really believe and to nurture that belief into the spiritual expression that is the product of your individual relationship with the divine, no matter how you perceive it.

If you have been a victim of any kind of religious trauma, take some time and answer the question. What would you still believe if heaven and hell were not part of the equation? What would you believe if you had not been disappointed or traumatized? You may be surprised that the answers to these two questions rarely match.

That is a far more sincere expression of your faith than is holding blindly to doctrines, prejudices, or standards that have been imposed either from pastors, elders, other leaders or even just by what appears to be a consensus among the people in your church.

If your belief causes you to fear, then soften it up a bit. It is yours. Be honest with yourself. The bible may say that the fear (awe) of the Lord is the beginning of wisdom, but it can also be the end of it if you do not grow in your own spiritual expression.

 No one needs to know what your core belief is. God already knows it and is waiting patiently for you to be honest with Him, but more importantly, honest with yourself.

Chapter 6

Not Stupid, Just Sincere

Belief is not stupid. It is essential for our survival and our wellbeing. I am not necessarily speaking of religious belief but belief as a mental process. It is critical to understand that humans are believing beings. The function of our memory is not to remember facts but to categorize our experiences in such a way that we *believe* we can accurately predict what might happen in any situation we face. For the most part, these memories are unconscious.

In fact, psychological science has demonstrated that each time a person consciously recalls a memory, less significant details may well have been forgotten and replaced with details we think of as more significant. In effect, every time we recall something, we lose a little of the mundane facts and expand on details that seem to fit better based on our experiences before and since the event occurred.

Let me give you a simple example from my own life. In my decision to move to Japan, the only way I remember what year it was, without looking at my resume, is that originally, I was supposed to go to Kuwait and that the Iraqis invaded Kuwait about a month before I left. Iraq invaded Kuwait in August. I was in Japan in September. It felt like a quick maneuver at the very last minute, a Hail Mary career move if there ever was one.

There had to be a series of events that had to take place for the change to happen but, I recall extraordinarily few of them. I find it impossible to reconstruct a legitimate timeline. Every time I try to put the timeline together, some detail that I think I remember does not logically fit and I find myself trying to figure out what happened based on what must have happened, not necessarily facts that I remember. The perceptions that remain are that events happened quickly, seamlessly, and seemingly at the last minute.

Have you ever recalled an event that you shared with another person and their recollection is distinctly different from your own?

Often victims of religious trauma have the same difficulty. Many of the elements or events that eventually led up to our trauma were small details that may have seemed insignificant at the time because our belief glossed over them. We may have excused them at the time. We may have ignored them because they did not fit our understanding. Often enough, we have explained or rationalized them away so that something that may have been significant was dismissed as pointless.

People who have never been in our situation have a difficult time understanding why we would excuse, ignore, or explain away what to them are obvious signs of something being amiss. They see our experience from the outside looking in. To them, the things we believed often seem irrational because they did not share the experiences that led to our particular belief.

You may be familiar with the Joe Rogan podcast. In many ways, Joe Rogan reminds me of Russel Brand in that they both have the highest possible opinion about their point of view. I admire them both, even if I do not always agree with them. I think we all should value our own opinions a bit more, especially after an experience of religious trauma.

We have to understand that at the time, we believed what we believed. When we were excusing, ignoring, or explaining away events that may have caused a little uneasy faith, we were doing exactly what makes us human and using what we perceived as the most relevant information available.

I bring up Joe Rogan because of an interview he conducted with Leah Remini, the actress who left Scientology after a long string of events which she admits she excused, ignored, or explained away. In the interview, Rogan persistently asked what moment or event triggered Remini to realize that she needed to leave Scientology.

Remini, who had been raised in the organization, tried to help Rogan understand that the trigger was not a single moment but a gentle series of far less significant elements that eventually led to her decision to leave. It was not *the* single straw that broke the camel's back but the mounting weight of all the straws.

How many times have I asked myself questions like Rogan posed to Remini? *Why didn't I leave when such-n-such happened? Why didn't I see what was wrong?*

I did not see what was wrong because I could not believe that something was wrong. At some point, the stacking of ignored events and the cumulative effects of uneasy faith shifts in our perception, and suddenly, we see it. When we finally see it, we are in so deep that doing anything about it potentially renders the trauma more severe. In fact, it may well create the main trauma.

Remini insistently tried to get Rogan to understand that she actually believed in Scientology. And when she describes her underlying reasons for doing the things she did as a Scientologist, one can only determine that she did them with the best of intentions. In her mind, she was saving the world, making the world a better place, and in her way, helping all the people who were not yet Scientologists. She was part of the work that would prevent the destruction to which the world was headed.

Does this sound familiar to you? Let's revisit the last paragraph but replace Scientology with Christian jargon. In his mind, he was doing the work of God. As a Christian, he was part of God's plan for our lives. He was working to make the world a kinder, happier, more Christian place. He was inspiring unbelievers to accept Jesus in preparation for His eventual return and perhaps helping many avoid the tribulation to come. What better motives are there?

Apparently, the flaws of Scientology were and are completely obvious to Rogan, and he had difficulty understanding her point. He might have intellectually ascended to what she said but his persistence demonstrated that he did not understand her position.

There is no shame in having believed something. Whether you believe the pyramids were built by aliens or monsters lurk under your bed, those beliefs come from your past perceptions of the world and the series of events that led up to your belief. To some, these beliefs seem irrational to the point of absurdity. It is not that they will not listen but that they cannot understand your position.

Just the way that the three months that passed prior to my going to Japan have become a blur that I try to understand, many church doctrines were created in the same process. We have no church records that existed prior to about 300 years after Christ. Much of what we think of as standard Christianity is a reconstruction of what must have been in order for us to arrive at the conclusion we have. This *history* is based almost entirely on perceptions of those who won the political battle when Constantine made Christianity the national religion of Rome. Discoveries of alternative texts such as those found in Nag Hamadi, are conveniently explained away in terms of the dominating view of Christianity, assuming it to be the right one.

We think of perpetrators of religious trauma to be evil-intended, malicious, and manipulative. Manipulative they may be, we must acknowledge that the malicious intent may be questionable.

Religion, particularly Christianity, but most religions in general function like a spiritual pyramid scheme. Often, the longer one remains in, the greater the investment and the higher the benefit. Rimini points out that some of the higher-ranking celebrity adherents to Scientology would find leaving the group unthinkable because they have it so good. As investment increases, the more one has to lose by failing to excuse, ignore or explain away inconsistencies.

In the cult from which I was shunned, the pastor had a hunger for power. He used his spiritual influence to convince heterosexual, mostly married men of the congregation to agree to sexual activities with him.

The sexual activities of that pastor were uncovered several times. Each time it was uncovered, some people left the organization and others, either excused or explained away his behavior, usually in the name of forgiveness in the light of his apparent repentance. That is what many other people and I did when we heard of it.

The first time I had a hint of the pastor's illicit behavior, was from a friend who told me that he had been approached to be a "special friend" of the pastor. He told me that that pastor's invitation to friendship felt creepy. I knew my friend was gay and I thought he was reading too much into the offer of friendship. I dismissed the thought, assured him that what he had to be wrong.

He was not wrong.

In other words, I excused, ignored, and explained away what should have alerted me to a real problem. And from my friend, I publicly ask for forgiveness because in reacting the way I did, I fear I may have hurt him. I at least left him alone in a situation that should have solicited comfort, not dismissal.

One Sunday after the service everyone who considered themselves a member of the church was invited to a meeting in the church social hall. The behavior of the pastor was exposed, and the elders told us that he had repented and that they believed him. I wanted to believe him, and I trusted them. We were invited to decide about staying or leaving the group, "with no hard feelings." I was invested and wanted to stay. Hard feelings or not, we did not associate much with the people who had left the congregation.

One of the women in the church who was a student at the same time I was and who displayed a similar tolerance for inconsistency, remained in the congregation after graduation. Years later, when her son, a handsome young man of high school age, was approached by the pastor, he did not give in but rather told his parents what he thought had been happening in his private moments with the pastor. She and her husband vowed to remain in the congregation until the pastor was ousted. I cannot tell you how much I admire them for that decision.

Joseph A. Onesta

Chapter 7

Desert Steps

Though my destination had morphed from Kuwait to Japan, I still saw the next year or so of my life as being alone in an unchristian wilderness. I intended it to be my time to pull myself together and see what God had instore for me. Thinking of Jesus' time in the desert before beginning his public ministry, I expected temptations and challenges. I chose to avoid speculating on what they might be because the thought of them scared me. I was confident, however, that God would never look away.

I tied up as many loose ends in New York as I could. I bade farewell to the people I loved and accepted the well-wishes from everyone who loved me. There were a few people who objected to my leaving. One woman, in particular, an amusingly insane woman, followed me through the apartment I shared with her niece and family, telling me that God had told her that the devil was after my soul. *Old news*, I thought, but I thanked her anyway.

Extended good-byes get old and tedious. There comes a time, when people start thinking, *Just go already!* So, I decided to spend the

53

last six weeks of my remaining summer break in Los Angeles. I had vaguely considered applying to grad school there. I imagined joining the folks at Church on the Way and perhaps continuing ministry there. I thought it would be good to get my bearings and it would get me away from New York.

I spent my first week with an old college friend in his apartment in North Hollywood, not too far from Church on the Way. He worked a lot, but we spent the evenings together tooling around Los Angeles and reminiscing. While he worked, I took my bible out to the pool with a cup of coffee. I read, had my quiet time, and spoke to God about my excitement about spending the next year getting closer to Him, and the adventure of living in a foreign country for which four months of studying Arabic had been rendered absolutely useless. When Iraq invaded Kuwait in August of that year, I was grateful for His provision of an alternative job, thus saving me from what might well have been a life-threatening adventure in Kuwait.

My friend was scheduled to leave for a planned trip to England about a week into my stay. He generously offered me keys to his apartment and his car while he was away, but I declined. Dillon and Michael had heard from Michael's brother that I would be returning to Los Angeles before going abroad and they offered their hospitality. Anyone in their right mind would choose several weeks in Venice Beach over being alone in an apartment in North Hollywood.

I do not know what went through Jesus' mind before he first stepped into the desert, but I suspect he was thinking much the same as I was. *Am I ready to be alone? Am I ready to accept God's will, no matter what? Would I be better prepared for ministry when I finished my journey?* I wondered if I might end up in my own garden of Gethsemane, asking for the cup from which I was to drink to pass me by.

54

Dillon and Michael were the perfect hosts. Again, I got to spend my days walking along the beach, seeing the sights. Dillon worked only until three or four in the afternoon. Michael did not get home until after six. I helped Dillon with the grocery shopping or running errands in the afternoon.

On one afternoon excursion, we went a place called *Smart and Final Iris*, a kind of restaurant supply store that was open to the public. Dillon had a list and was buying items that seemed out of character. There were large quantities of meat, milk vegetables, and fruit. There were also things like candy, chips, and soda, which were unusual items for them.

"What's the occasion?" I asked.

Dillon explained the list was from a group home that catered to teenage runaways who had been thrown out of their family homes because they were gay. The group home provided food and shelter. Tutors volunteered to help the kids who enrolled in school and the charity had counselors to help the kids with emotional and psychological issues. Ultimately, they hoped to find long-term, foster homes for the kids. Until stable homes could be found, the kids lived in the group home. Dillon and Michael bought a week's worth of groceries and supplies once every two or three months.

"No offense but you might be surprised how unreasonably cruel some Christian families can be," he said.

"I'm afraid it would not surprise me at all," I muttered. I knew Dillon heard me, but he did not respond. He only smiled.

During one of our afternoons together, Dillon brought up my coming out again and this time, I confided in him. He listed carefully to how I expressed the conflict I had been experiencing.

"I thought as much.," he confirmed. As it turned out, Dillon had grown up in an Evangelical family in Oklahoma and understood me perfectly.

It was really good to be able to talk to someone openly and without fearing how the conversation might affect how the other person related to me. Dillon asked personal questions, but I did not mind. He asked me about my sexual experience. When had I first suspected that I was attracted men and was I attracted to women as well? How many other gay people did I know and what were they like? He even asked me what records I had broken after the Tomczak event.

"Well, my dear, it seems you do not have enough information to go on. May I suggest we visit a few gay venues while you are here, just so you know more about the gay community?"

The first place we visited was the Gay and Lesbian Community Center and perused the bulletin board for activities that might be of interest. I was amazed at the variety but there was nothing for me.

We spent an afternoon volunteering at an agency that helped people with AIDS. They were planning a fundraising event and we helped to fill gift bags with designer freebees for the guests who would have not only paid a generous sum for their dinner but who fully expected to be asked to write a big check. That was fun.

We also visited a number of restaurants, coffee shops, bars and clubs that catered to the gay community. One evening, we went to a gay West Hollywood club called Micky's. Until then, I had maintained observer status around gay people. How much like or unlike these people was I? I saw some things I did not like but none of them seemed to be the Sodom and Gomorrah I had expected. I grew increasingly comfortable and some of the people I met were very nice.

That night, I noticed an exceptionally attractive guy. I could not take my eyes off him. I watched him dance. I watched him move. He was astonishingly handsome. He was clearly in his element. He was confident. And he seemed to be alone. Eventually, I mustered the nerve to approach him and ask him to dance with me.

I had never approached a man that way before. In fact, that was the first time I had ever asked anyone to dance with me who was not someone I had already known as a friend. His name was Danel. That is not a typo; he was Basque. He had newly arrived in Los Angeles on a teacher exchange program. He was easy to talk to and comfortable to be with. He laughed at some of the terms I learned to use in my time at the church in the Bronx. He said they were archaic terms that people no longer used very much. I thought his Spanish was beautiful to listen to. His pronunciation and the tone of his voice were warm and calming.

We were still together when Dillon and Michael mentioned meeting other friends at *The Abbey*, a coffee shop around the corner. Though we sat with five or six people, it felt as if Danel and I were alone. Before we left for the night, Danel pulled me aside and asked me to go back to his apartment with him. He lived near Michael and Dillon, so I knew I would have an escape route if unexpectedly he turned out to be creepy. To be honest, though, I really wanted to go with him. I accepted and we remained together almost constantly until I left for Japan about a month later.

I did not much recriminate myself for having sex with Danel. I experienced some conflict, but I believed that being with him was something I needed to do. After all, we were both consenting adults. I enjoyed his company and I enjoyed him physically. Given my previous, even remotely sexual encounters, which had all be traumatic in some way, my experience with Danel was really beautiful. He was kind, gentle and affectionate. He was a bit more passionate than I had anticipated, and his passion made me feel like he wanted to be with me, not just have sex, but to be with me. For the first time in my life, I felt desirable.

Part of me used the brief relationship to gauge my ability to be in that life. It was also safe because I would be on a plane to Japan in just a few weeks. As much as I liked Danel and believed that I could be with him for the rest of my life, part of me knew that it was temporary. I was aware that I was also experiencing something important to my own development. He was, after all, the first. I had had crushes before but never like that. After the event with Tomczak, I never allowed the crushes to linger. I had been engaged to a beautiful woman for about a year, but frankly, we both thought that being together was God's will more than either of us was in love with the other.

Danel was a delight, and we had a good time. One evening we attended a B52s AIDS benefit concert at the Great Western Forum. I had hardly heard of the B52s and I was still into Christian music almost exclusively. Our seats were on the floor of the forum, close enough to the stage to see the musicians clearly. I thoroughly enjoyed the concert though I could not sing along the way other attendees did.

After the concert, as we climbed the stairs between the seats toward the exits, there was a bit of a traffic jam ahead. We came upon a man sitting on the steps. Other concertgoers stepped around and some, even over him.

I bent down and asked him if he was alright?

"I'm fine," he said. "The climb is a little too much for me."

I offered him my shoulder. At first, he refused but I insisted. "You can't just sit here. Come on!" I helped him stand and Danel and I half carried him up the stairs.

As we separated in the parking lot, he thanked us for our kindness. He mentioned that he had AIDS, that he had come alone to the concert and was glad to meet both of us.

The juxtaposition of the AIDS benefit concert and the fact that people just walked around this man in his distress struck me. At the time, many people would have feared the contact we had shared climbing the stairs. We did not know then as much then about AIDS as we did even a few years later. In most circles, people who had AIDS were the contemporary version of lepers. In hindsight, he may have felt morally obliged to tell us of his status.

I completely connected with God using me to help someone He loved very dearly. It was an honor. I said nothing to Danel. He knew I was religious, but spirituality was not something we shared.

The first of my desert temptations came quickly. It happened as I was leaving for Japan. The several weeks with Danel had affected me more than I had thought. We sat together in the airport, waiting for my flight. He kept looking away and wiping tears from his eyes. I almost did not board the plane.

I had an eleven-hour flight in which to contemplate my experience with Danel and process the pain of leaving him. At that, it was not enough. It took several months.

I cannot say that I had actually fallen in love. Though I was twenty-nine years old, that was the first real relationship I had ever had, however brief it was. It was also the first time I had made love to anyone.

Though I had been engaged to an unbelievably beautiful woman, there was a lesson in Danel for me regarding that relationship. I understood that I could not ever have felt about her the way I felt when I was with Danel. I just was not built that way. She deserved to truly be desired the way I felt that Danel desired me. In the Bible, Jacob labored fourteen years to marry Rachel and the children she bore him, Joseph and Benjamin, had been his favorites. No matter how Godly or Christ-centered our married life would have been, that essential element would have been distinctly absent.

Still, I was not ready to declare myself gay. I had had one brief gay relationship, but I was not ready for that step. I also knew that I could never pretend to be straight to be with a woman because it would amount to an act and attitude of deception. I would have to be celibate or gay. I knew I could not love a woman the way I could love a man.

For perhaps six months, I ruminated over Danel almost constantly. He and our brief relationship was a kind of anchor for me. Gradually, our correspondence waned, and the puppy love I felt for him faded.

God has always known about my sexuality. He was not testing me with Danel to see what I would do. After all, He knew what I would do with Danel before I had done it. He saw me in my struggle. I had long believed He loved me despite my struggle. I began to see that His love for me was profound *through* my struggle. He knew and understood the emotions I was having and the loss I felt as I boarded that plane. What he wanted for me at that moment was comfort, not rebuke. I am the man God made me and while I cannot be proud of every aspect of my life, I do not need to be ashamed of them either.

For months, my meditations were on acceptance, loving-kindness, and grace. That worked into a different understanding of sin and sins. I abandoned keeping lists of sins and began considering the quality and nature of what might be sinful, why it my be sinful.

When I was a young Catholic boy, lists of sins were all I had to go on. I used to have to confess my sins to a priest. I remember being terrified if, in the confessional, I had forgotten to mention something. Eventually, when I told the priest I was afraid that I might have forgotten something, he absolved me anyway and said I could always add the phrase, ". . .and any sin I may have forgotten." He must have been amused at that.

Today, I have a relationship with the Holy Spirit who easily convicts me when I have done something that has harmed another person or perhaps was motivated by something other than love. Whether I did it intentionally, in a moment of pique or completely unwittingly, there is a still but firm voice that shows me how I might grow in love and thus grow in God. (1 John 4:7)

Chapter 8

Eyes Wide Open

I have always prayed with my eyes open. I feel less connected to God with my eyes closed. It is a habit that has strengthened over the years. I can only guess at the reason this characteristic remains with me. My earliest memories of church are standing on the pew as everyone around me was kneeling in a very ornate, quite beautiful, tiny Roman Catholic church. I was probably three or four. The prayer was in a language I did not really understand. I am guessing it was Latin as adults frequently spoke Italian to one another at home.

I remember standing there looking above the people at the building, the heavy stone walls, the stained-glass windows, and the banks of candles.

Even growing up, when I was kneeling with everyone else, I never closed my eyes. When we said grace before a meal and even when I was saying my nightly prayers, my eyes were open.

For about a year in high school, strange things were happening in my bedroom. Things would move and sometimes I would even see them moving. There was an oppressive cold that would come over the room when I went to bed. Perhaps these phenomena could have been explained rationally. But there were no pets nor pests to move things. The cold would come on suddenly as if someone had turned on strong air-conditioning, but we did not have air-conditioning. I cannot explain it. It felt oppressive and scary.

I confided in a few friends who gifted me with Catholic medals, a scapular, and the text of St. Michael's prayer. Every night, as I got into bed, I recited a number of prayers beginning and ending with St. Michael. Eyes wide open, sensitive, and perceiving both the atmosphere and the environment. As I prayed, the creepy feeling would fade, the room would warm comfortably and there would be no more surprises. I could then fall asleep.

Those prayers were really my recitation of composed prayers, which became almost automatic, much the way many pray The Lord's Prayer. They operated for me like a kind of mantra or, in hypnosis, we might say an induction. They put me in a meditative state through which my conscious and unconscious minds were united in purpose.

Devil, demon, or delusion, I cannot tell but those medals and scapular hung around my neck for years until my Evangelical and Pentecostal friends convinced me to take them off. I always continued to pray, always with my eyes open and always experiencing a wonderful sense of connecting with divinity, beyond time and space.

When I would pray with others, I would follow the instruction to close my eyes and bow my head but only for the first minute or two. Soon, I would be looking around the room, at the décor perhaps, at my brothers and sisters in Christ, at the expressions on their faces, and sensing the atmosphere that changed when the prayer began and always part of me focusing on the intentions of the prayer. For a long time, I felt as if my prayer life did not measure up, was not of equal caliber to that of others because my eyes were open. It was a silly thought, but I had it.

Later, the quality of my prayer life is what carried me through. It was not in the words we uttered but in that attention on and contact with the divine. On one occasion when it was my turn to say grace at dinner, once I had focused my attention on that communication, all I could say was "amen." Grace that evening was three or for amens with pauses in between. I got teased for that, but I did not mind.

Prayer provided me with a grounding element that kept me from fleeing the church. It still keeps me abandoning my spirituality. Prayer was and remains my most consistent expression of my connection to the divine.

You will judge me as you will. I have learned and become comfortable with the judgment of Christians because they are apt to do it whether I like it or not. Whether the judgment is meant to be productive, or it turns out to be destructive, it says more about their relationship with God than it says about mine. No one, absolutely no one, except for God himself, has the right to criticize or evaluate my spiritual expression.

When I lived in New York, the local laundromat was run by a woman who was happy to move my clothes from the washer to the dryer if my visit to the bagel shop or the grocery store took too long. She was a nice lady but full of gossip. People often stopped into the laundromat just to greet her and catch up on the neighborhood news.

One day, as I sat waiting for my dryer to finish, I heard her say something that caught my attention and made me think. She had pointed to a couple walking by the window and began elaborating how flirtatious the man behaved when his wife was not around. "He's always looking for another place to dip his stick," She said using a crude but effective euphemism. "And as for her, all I can say is love is blind but the neighbors ain't."

I wondered if that woman was just willfully blind. Had she never heard the rumors about her husband? Had she never discovered his flirtatious behavior if it were true? Had there perhaps been at least one neighbor who tried to alert her to her husband's infidelity? Was she satisfied with her marriage? If he had heard the rumors, why did not she confront the gossips or perhaps more appropriately, her husband. If she knew they were true, why did she stay with him? Exactly how much about her marriage did any of the gossips really know? They may think she stayed with him because she was stupid. Or, perhaps she did not respect herself enough to stand up to him? It was just as likely that she had no choice, did not care, or had no objection to her husband's activities. Maybe she like his flirtatious nature. Maybe he was not doing as much dipping of the stick as it seemed. Maybe they would have been less critical if he had been flirtatious with them.

When we criticize the spiritual expression of another, we invalidate it and often invalidate them at the same time.

In the parable of the prodigal son, the father gave his child all the latitude he desired. Of course, the father knew the son well and knew he would likely squander his inheritance. No doubt the father hoped for the son's return and when it eventually happened, he celebrated. He had never ceased to be the young man's father and in the end, he not only got his son back, but the son was wiser than when he had first taken leave.

The other son, the one who had remained faithful to his father complained at the injustice he perceived. The inherent mandate in fairness and human justice seem obvious here but when mandate and love conflict, we should just let love win.

I am not prescribing or even hinting that anyone should pray with their eyes open or that they should attempt to feel or experience what I experience in prayer. There is nothing prescriptive here, only descriptive. But I have two points to make. First, blindly following mandates is not faith but fear. Blind faith is fear. We should approach all aspects of our faith with our eyes open. Second, no one, absolutely no one, has the right to invalidate the spiritual expression of anyone else, period.

Blind faith often creates uneasy faith. One of the most significant sources of mounting religious trauma is not seeing or not paying attention to the signs that something is wrong. Perhaps it is an event, something someone says, an announced decision or a pastor invites someone to be his "special friend." Whatever it may be, it just does not sit right. We may choose to see these instances as insignificant at the time. We may simply brush them aside because paying attention to them is difficult, awkward, or possibly painful. If the problem persists, we may try our best to explain it away until it becomes so obvious that something just snaps, and things fall apart, and we are emotionally swept away with the debris.

When setting out on a journey, we often have an image of our destination in mind. When we finally reach that destination, we may be disappointed because it does not measure up to the ideal our imagination conjured. Instead, perhaps it's better to treat life's journeys the way I experience a new place when I travel. I have a destination in mind but know that if I only focus on the destination and pay no attention to what I encounter along the way, I will miss a lot. The destination merely provides the direction in which I travel. If I get there it does not matter if the destination is wonderful or turns out disappointing. I still have all that I discovered along the way.

No matter how far we travel, the horizon still exists. The horizon never gets any closer.

A few years ago, as I visited one of my brothers from the college fellowship. Disparagingly he remarked that my spiritual perspective had changed. He was intimating that I my spiritual life had been sullied. "Matured," I countered. "It would be a shame if I had remained the same person in my fifties as I was at nineteen." I am sorry to say he did not agree with my assessment. He saw his adherence as staying faithful and I saw my change as maturation.

My eyes remain open. I see no value only disillusionment in blind faith.

Chapter 9

Rabbi for an Hour

There are some Christian sects that believe we can obtain perfection in this life, that if we believe the right things, submit ourselves to God's will and if we work hard enough, we can become perfect in this life. The idea is absurd.

While most Christians can admit that they are not perfect now and are unlikely to ever approach perfection on earth, we seem to expect perfection of our pastors, teachers, elders, and preachers. And too many of us quietly demand it of ourselves while never living up to the exemplars we think we should be.

Whether it is out of disappointment, shame or we are just buying time, many of us wear a kind of Christian mask. We pretend. We fake it until we make it. Perhaps in small, extremely confidential circles, we might admit to weakness. Our reticence if understandable, if not completely justifiable.

When as a young man I confided my same-sex attraction to my brothers in small group bible study, something between us changed.

Perhaps they were uncomfortable Perhaps they thought it was contagious. Perhaps they thought I had a demon. I am not sure the reason but there was more distance between us after my confession than before.

I was also shocked and dismayed at how quickly word spread beyond our little group. I had hoped for help, understanding and support and what I got was nothing of the sort. If I choose to think the best of them, the leaders did not know what to do with me and themselves sought counsel. If I choose to think the worst of them, those in the group may well have engaged in salacious gossip.

How can I be sure the news spread? Everything changed. Clandestinely, a number of people came forward to let me know they shared the same struggle and perhaps it was a mistake to open up about it. Those conversations were so brief, they could hardly be called support.

More to the point, I acquired a label that inhibited or tailored how nearly everyone else saw me. After my confession, I doubt that I would have been selected for any position of responsibility and the following academic year, I was placed in a different fellowship house as if perhaps, after my tiny excursion to a bar, and now this new information, they would feel more comfortable with me at a distance.

It is strange that I remember my roommates from the first house but do not remember my roommates from the second. In reaction to the shift in attitude, I spent truly little free time in that house and less in my bedroom. I did little more than sleep there and attend the mandatory meetings around worship, breakfast, and dinner. I learned very quickly that instead of support, I gained segregation and isolation. It was easier and more comfortable for me to study in the library. The worst part of that outcome was that I thought I deserved it. It is possible that I read too much into the shift I perceived but remember, we are beings whose belief is determined by our perceptions.

Intellectually, I never believed I would achieve perfection, but I just wanted to be better, always better, and never allowing myself the frailty that makes us human. It is unfortunate that we do not consider frailty and even failure an asset to a life of faith. Later, after my ordination, an event I considered to be recognition of my progress, I was shocked and disappointed that I could recognize no significant difference in my walk with God. I suffered from not only my personal struggle but my inability to recognize my own growth.

There are some clergy members who embody the exact opposite of the humility and vulnerability which I have come to value. Generously, I expect that some of them think they must be an example of piety to inspire the congregation. How can I judge them if such an idea had been a snare for me? A little less generously, I suspect some try to maintain the rouse of their own piety because they find the contrast between their practical lives and the example, they wish to set too striking and embarrassing. They are likely aware that they are being disingenuous but think it is just part of the job for the sake of others.

It takes no generosity on my part to acknowledge that at least some of them enjoy what the rouse gets them. Their mask is no longer for the benefit of those they instruct but for their own gain. They enjoy the position of honor at the table, the deference they receive, even the discounted prices they might get because people think they should be nice to clergy.

Perfection and overt piety are always a rouse. Assuming a position of honor is contrary to the teachings of Jesus. Overtly refusing an honor, false humility, is an equal expression of vanity. If you think the pastor should assume a place of honor, then I suggest spending a little time in Luke 14 and Proverbs 25.

I once observed a perfect example of humility. I attended the funeral of the father of a dear friend. It is the custom of the congregation for the church to host the lunch after the funeral. The parishioners prepare the food and donate both the food and their service.

After the service, we were invited to the social hall in the basement of the church. The food was set out on a buffet and the pastor who had officiated the funeral, said grace. I have been to a good many funerals in my sixty years and I had considered it a matter of course for the pastor and those seated at his table to be served first. When this pastor finished saying grace, he indicated a table of guests inviting them the buffet. After the line had begun, he occupied himself visiting each table and personally greeting guests. When the last table was in line, he took a plate and joined them. His behavior was an exemplary performance of humility, grace, and hospitality.

My own weaknesses had brought me to my knees, but precious few people knew what had prompted that posture. I expected the change that others said they saw and a change that I believed God had promised. I just had to get through that dark valley of my struggle. Until I attempted to resign from the ministry, I would have claimed that I well knew King David's valley of the shadow of death. (Psalm 23)

I saw myself as a man with a purpose, a mission. I had imagined myself married to a fine Christian woman with children of our own. I held an image of me grinding the gears of an old school bus full of third-world orphans, my wife and I giving them the love and guidance that absent parents could not.

When I left the church in the Bronx, I separated myself because I thought of myself as a contaminate, the way I did in my second fellowship housing assignment in college. There was something wrong with me that was incompatible with my idea of what a man of God was. In the desert, I eventually discovered that I was a man of God because of my weakness more than for my strengths. I learned to embrace my own humanity. One cannot be a man or woman of God without first being at peace about being human.

My flight to Osaka Airport from Los Angeles landed a few hours earlier than the rest of the faculty flying in from New York. With hours to spare, I wandered the airport. I had only two phrases in Japanese. I could ask for a cup of coffee. I could ask where the bathroom was but could not understand the directions to it.

Like me, about half the faculty were beginning their first semester in Japan. Although I had taught at various campuses of City University of New York, I did not know any of them well. They were an interesting group, mostly native New Yorkers; some of them were experienced in teaching English as a Second Language, I had known some of their names from rosters, but we had not had much contact with one another. The instructors and professors of general education subjects, humanities, sociology, anthropology, history, were complete strangers to me.

During the first week on campus, there were scheduled activities. Small groups of us were taken to open bank accounts and go to the grocery store. One poor instructor, thinking she had bought hand cream, swathed her hands and arms with mayonnaise. Another, thinking he had bought sugar, later gagged on the saltiest cup of coffee known to man. But we settled in, and the semester began. There was a chapel on campus that went unused. I thought I might ask for a key but decided that I would have better quiet times either in my apartment or walking the lanes of the rural town. The Hiroshima countryside is quite picturesque and lush. More than once a well-meaning towns person stopped their car and insisted that I board. Thinking I was lost, they would bring me back to campus until I learned how to say, *"Gomennasai, Daijoubu desu. Sanpo shiteimasu"* (*It's OK, I'm just out for a stroll.*)

I said nothing about being a minister or about being gay. I made friends but decided to keep my private life to myself

My being a minister was listed on my Curriculum Vitae and I suspect that is how my fellow faculty members eventually learned that I had religious credentials. One day, a married couple, also on faculty, approached me about leading a Jewish Kaddish service in memory of their little daughter who had died one year earlier. There was no rabbi, and I was the closest thing they could find.

Ringing in my ears was the phrase the senior pastor had said to me before I left, "The gifts and calling of God are irrevocable." But I was not being called on to be a minister. I was being called to fill a role I did not know how to play, except as a compassionate human with some ministry experience. I wanted to refuse but my heart would not let me. I agreed to do it, but I did not know how to conduct a Jewish Kaddish service. Of course, I understood that mentioning Jesus in the service would not be kosher. The closest thing to a Jewish service I had ever attended was a Yom Kippur service run by Jews for Jesus. I had no idea how typical that service had been.

I cannot describe my initial feelings about conducting a service without using the name of Jesus. It was a real problem for me, and I spent much time praying about how to handle it. One evening in one of my walks during which I had walked far enough from campus that I earnestly wished some local villager would offer me a ride, I had a flash of understanding.

I was not being tempted in the desert, but my dogmas, my doctrines, were being challenged. I saw how holding to my dogmas and doctrines actually limited my ability to be a minister, specifically in this case. While I wanted to get my head clear about my sexuality, God had a different goal in mind. He was giving me problems to face, problems that would broaden and deepen my ability to minister, if I chose to rise to the call.

The first challenge had come with Danel. Danel was not a temptation to see if I would embrace homosexuality, but rather a challenge to my idea of what it meant to be a man of God. As a result of Danel, I had come to realize that I could never love a woman the way I could love another man. Thus, one major obstacle to my moving forward had been removed. I no longer had to think of marriage to a woman which meant I really did not have to think much about God making me a heterosexual. There would never be a pastor's wife in my life. The image I had of a man of God, married with children is irrevocably altered. Ethically, I could not marry a woman believing that she deserved a husband who appropriately desired her. She should not be denied the feeling of being desired. Since marrying a man was impossible, celibacy was the only alternative that remained.

75

I put it before God and told him I would be willing to be willing to accept a celibate life. I laughed to myself because I thought of Augustine who, in is memoire admitted to praying, "Lord, make me chaste, but not yet." The odd thing was is that I had no intention of looking for sex but having met Danel, I was willing to be willing. That was the best I could offer with integrity.

The Kaddish episode was another challenge, one that was teaching me what it meant to be a minister. As I walked the long walk home, it started to rain a heavy soaking rain. It was chilly. I was quickly soaked to the point my footsteps squished. But my mind was in a different dimension entirely. If I were to be a minister, I would need to be a minister to everyone, not just to those who thought like me. I had to be ready for anyone who needed me.

In 1 Corinthians 9:19-23, Paul recounts almost the same experience except he seemed to focus on *conversion*. His point was converting everyone he met. I admit, until my soggy walk home, I had understood salvation mostly in terms of conversion. Perhaps that was what Paul meant at the time, but salvation had suddenly become so much more than conversion in my thinking.

Jesus loved that couple and their little girl as much as he loved me and anyone else. They were in mourning and deserved love, compassion, and sympathy. They deserved ministry. I was able to proceed with the service with a clear conscience, expressing God's love without being a dogmatic ass about my faith.

The couple gave me a few photos of their little girl. As I prayerfully studied these photos, I tried to imagine the little girl in life. I could almost hear her giggle and chatter as children do. Empathically, I could sense the confusion the parents felt, the fear, the frustration, and perhaps even the sense of abandonment. How they must have hoped, prayed, even pleaded for the miracle of her recovery and the disappointment when their delightful little girl left this world. Having no children of my own, knowing then that I would never have children of my own, I could only vaguely imagine the pain of the loss of a child. I would do all I could to comfort them. If that meant a service, a service they would have and the best service I could offer.

Personally, I felt humbled and honored at the same time. It felt like being ordained again, this time as rabbi for an hour. The truth was, they could have conducted the service without me. They did not need me at all. There were at least ten Jewish men on faculty. They had a minyan without me and technically, my ordination should have meant little to them. It was a most undeserved honor and privilege to mourn the loss of that little girl and be of some comfort to her grieving parents.

I led the service as I would have done a Christian one with some minor exceptions. Some other faculty members came to my rescue by transliterating the Kaddish prayer. All I had to do was start the prayer and they would pick it up.

Yitgadal v'yitkadash . . .

At the end of the service, I raised my hands as I would normally do to bless the congregation. I had no idea if rabbis did such a thing. I had not thought to ask anyone. I prayed over them sending them on their way with the blessings of God.

For the first time in my life, I had officiated a service without using the name of Jesus, who, let us not forget, was thoroughly Jewish and who, with his disciples, had more than a minyan on their own. For many of my readers, even the thought of doing such a thing might seem disingenuous at best, seditious at worst. But I understood that I was a minister of God and God cares about everyone.

The couple approached me later and thanked me for the service. They were touched and commented that at the moment I raised my hands to bless the congregation, they felt something wonderful. At home, in a private moment with God, I wept in gratitude for the grace that had been extended to me. I realize in some way that I had passed my second challenge. I also recognized that God ministers to his beloved children, all of us, anyway he can, anyway we will receive his nurturing. To be a true minister of the divine, we must understand love and be willing to be its vessel.

Spirituality is supposed to nurture you, inform your life like a loving parent gently guides a child. Spirituality is a way of knowing what your true core values are.

Unfortunately, we have manipulated religion to the point of making it mere dogma. We have idolized religion, both dogmas, and doctrines, to the point that if someone is going to fit in, they have to become like us. They have to act like us. They have to use the same words we do. They ultimately have to think like us. Some have humorously called this behavior, cookie-cutter Christianity. But there is nothing funny about it. (Matthew 23:27, Romans 2:24)

Cookie-cutter Christianity is not true spirituality but a cheap imitation. This form of traditional Christianity reminds me of foundry workers creating sand molds that will receive molten metal. Once the metal is poured and cooled enough, the sand is broken away to reveal a rough version of the object. Then a machinist takes the casting and grinds off all the rough spots. The result is nearly identical objects with only the most minor differences.

You might now be thinking of Proverbs 27:17. Look it up if you do not know the verse by heart. May I suggest the verse is not about conforming to a norm but rather the establishment of an organic, natural relationship between people of mutual and self-respect.

One cool autumn day, walking on Orchard Beach just outside of New York City, I stumbled upon a patch of what looked like scorched sand. It was a spot where lightning had struck a metal object. I do not know what the object had been, but it was more substantial than an aluminum can. It had perhaps been a rod either cast or extruded aluminum. How it got there and why it was half buried in the sand is even beyond speculation. The sand around the scorch mark was a discolored and pitted small crater. I decided to explore it. As I dug the metal object out of the sand, it went much deeper than I had expected. The form I eventually pulled out of the sand was beautiful, complex, smooth in some places, rough in others. It was impossible to bend but the shape twisted, turned unpredictably, almost melodically.

This is what true spirituality is for me. An expression of power from the lightening touching the metal, with all its fundamental properties, melting and becoming solid once again, in the environment of resisting and shifting sand, never again the be the same, forever changed, the intricacies of which require longer than a lifetime to fully appreciate. It is an exquisite melding of the divine and the mundane.

When I am working with someone who has experienced religious trauma, I feel very much like I felt that day on Orchard Beach, as if we are engaged in a process of discovery. We talk a lot, use hypnotic techniques to relax and we discover at first that tiny seed of belief, whatever it is. As we nurture it, it takes shape organically. With proper nurturing, a genuine work of art will emerge having its own unique beauty and elegance.

Sometimes, my clients ask me to pray with them. I agree to do so only if they lead the prayer. I have long since left the job of influencing others what to believe and thus, how to interact with the divine. I can agree with them in prayer on almost anything in any way they express it. Given their traumatic experience, I would not want lead in prayer simply because I do not know how they might react no do I know how they might understand my words, clear though they may be to me.

Chapter 10

Believing Changes You

Have you ever wondered about how some Christians could be so harsh, cruel, priggish, and legalistic? It is because that is how they see Jesus. Perhaps they came to Jesus after a hellfire and brimstone sermon, or they grew up being threatened with hell and damnation if they did not behave, as if God dealt out heavenly rewards the way Santa Clause gives gifts at Christmas. Except for the fact that Santa is much more inclined to benevolence. I remember laughing at the character Maude in the old sitcom when she would look disapprovingly at her husband and say, "God will get you for that, Walter." It was funny because it was a sitcom. In real life, to a lot of people, such an idea is no joke.

One of the most legalistic Christians I have ever known experienced patterns of manic behavior that ranged from extreme fundamentalism to out-and-out debauchery. He would go through seasons of excessive drinking, drugs, and indiscriminate sexual behavior, to the point of losing his job, his car, and his home. When he finally hit bottom, Jesus would *save* him again, and he would spend a season quoting the Bible and condemning anyone who experienced more freedom than he did. I believe he needed the structure, not because of sin but because legalism had saved his life at least twice in our acquaintance. The last time I saw him, he was condemning me while living with a woman who was not his wife. Apparently, she was doing "God's work" by pulling his sorry butt out of the gutter.

Fear and frustration were central to his safety and survival. That is why he was so condemning of others who expressed freedom. I grew up drinking a small portion of wine, sometimes at Sunday dinner, sometimes a sip at church during communion, and always on holidays. Jesus at the wedding of Cana allegedly made some pretty strong wine (John 2:10). Wine was not a problem for me at all. For my friend, however, even a small amount of wine became a binge that led to his full-blown debauchery. He was clearly an alcoholic, and in his use of alcohol, he rationalized or dulled his feelings further with drugs and sex. As long as his fear of God reigned, he was less apt to engage in self-destructive behaviors. It seems for him, that 1 Corinthians 6:12 would prove to be a stumbling block.

The point is that we hear what we hear because of what we have already heard and believed. That belief effects in us behavior that seems to be evidence of what we actually believe. That is why, I encourage everyone to boil down their belief to its very essence, the very seed of faith—which is a form of belief. That faith will grow and take on its natural, (not prescribed) form. It will be pruned, nurtured, and eventually changed in some way, but that is a natural process. (1 Corinthians 13:11-13)

I am not going to go into a long, extensive, theological debate over major tenets of the Christian faith. As for that, we do not all agree even on those. But I will emphatically state that the way a Christian perceives and believes affects the kind of Christian they become. If they truly see God as vengeful, angry at sin and sinners who commit sins, then their expression of their faith is in line with that belief.

If they see God as a benevolent, loving, even indulgent father, they learn to extend that love to themselves, and then unconditionally toward others, not only other Christians but others in general.

As part of a theological exercise, I once studied the Apostle's Creed and took it verse by verse. The thing that I noticed was that the creed addressed the birth of Christ then, immediately jumped to his death. It was as if his teachings and life example were less important than those two events, namely, the virgin birth and the crucifixion and resurrection. In terms of theological stance, it was apparently more important to the writers to demonstrate the divinity of Christ and the propitiation or atonement of the cross than it was to live according to the teachings of Jesus. In the "works vs. faith" debate, doctrine is the deciding factor, while works pay a secondary role.

Legend suggests that the Apostles Creed was penned by the Apostles themselves before setting out on their individual ministries, ultimately ending with their martyrdom. I personally find it difficult to believe that they would leave out the actual teaching and life example of the man they followed.

When I began looking at the Nicene Creed with a critical eye, it was that very theology on steroids. The writers were making a statement about what one had to believe to be considered a Christian, thus eliminating anyone who disagreed with them on any point. Considering the purpose of the council at Nicaea, this was as much political posturing as it was theological.

Given the subsequent discord created by standardizing the creeds, I wonder if the reverse stance might be preferable. That is, living according to the example and teachings of Jesus, what we have of them, seems more indicative of being Christian, or "like Christ," than adhering to a theology which he himself never espoused.

Jesus spoke of knowing the nature of a tree by the fruit it produced. In other words, a sincere faith is evidenced by what the believer does rather than what the believer says. (Matthew7:15-20)

If you have been around Christians long enough, you have heard people debate whether or not a person can or cannot lose their salvation. Eventually the argument gets to the unanswerable question, *were people who have fallen away ever truly saved?* Eventually, moving to safer ground, someone will say something along the lines that being saved is not a license to sin. It is my contention that a person who believes does not need or want a license to sin. We all do or think or say things we should not. This is not due to a lack of faith or anyone claiming a license or right to sin. It is, however, wondrously human. Our acknowledgment of frailty and even failure, helps us keep it real. It ties us together and allows us to extend to each other the grace and forgiveness extended to us.

Life is not a qualification round for how we will spend eternity. If I am on a spiritual path, my destination is not heaven or hell. For the spiritual seeker, eternity has already begun. It starts here, on earth, in this life. Heaven and hell exist here already.

Take it from me, a clinical hypnotist who helps many people stop bruxism. There is plenty of "gnashing of teeth" in this life. It is when we take heaven and hell out of the equation that we are able to isolate and define the very seed of faith that can grow. Whatever you do, do not merely accept a doctrine because it has been stated to you, like a prescription the doctor says you need to take. Prescriptive doctrines have too many side effects.

If you have been injured in any way by the church, people in the church, a denomination, individual Christians, or, in your opinion, Christendom in general, your healthiest move is to take time and find your grain of truth, from which your spirituality will eventually grow.

The alternative is as emotionally and psychologically destructive as wine was for my friend. Trying to define yourself by what you do not believe, is toxic and caustic. Even atheists *believe* something they cannot prove. Belief is part of our nature. It is part of what makes us human. It is essential for our survival; otherwise, we cannot effectively function in the world in which we live. If we deny belief, we deny our very selves.

I do not believe anything merely because the Bible says so. I do not believe anything simply because an apparently more learned person says so. What I believe today is decidedly different than what I believed as a young man. I found that grain of truth, that seed of faith and nurtured it. It continues to grow and mature. I expect that it will do so until I leave this planet.

I have come to believe that calling the Bible the "word of God" actually does an injustice both to God and His message. If the word of God is living and active, then it cannot be adequately expressed in a codex of disconnected and unrelated works by multiple authors who are inconsistent in their message and whose works were pieced together by people jockeying for position in a political world.

The most original documents we have were penned some 300 years after the life of Christ. I do not know about you, but I could not recreate the stories my own mother told and retold within the span of my lifetime without adulterating them even slightly by how I understood the story when it was told. Why should we expect anything different from the people who penned the books of the bible?

If God inspired the Bible, rather than trying to make the bible conform to our doctrines, we should embrace the inherent ambiguities that are implied by the inconsistencies and contradictions because He allowed them to be there. Perhaps, just perhaps, those issues exist to give us the opportunity of grappling with them.

If the word of God is vibrant and influential (Hebrews 4:12), it is living and active *in people*, not a book, not a set of doctrines or dogmas and certainly not in the traditions of a church or denomination, especially when there are so many, and they disagree.

God knows the limits and the failings of the human hand and mind. Those failings do not threaten nor disturb God at all. We are not ever going to take God by surprise. He never tests us to see how we do.

You do not have to become a Bible scholar nor an expert in church history. You do not have to study Greek, Hebrew, Latin, or Aramaic. You do not need to repeat the words of the pastor, a teacher, or anyone else. If you choose to read your Bible, commune with God right where you are. If you decide to read something else or ponder the universe in your own way, do so.

It seems clear to me that Jesus, throughout his teachings, made something quite clear. Religiosity and overt pious expression were acts of hypocrisy displayed to impress other people while sincere contact with the divine effectively changes a person.

I am not a Christian because I profess to be. In fact, given the behavior of many vocal Christians, I would prefer not to be labeled among them. The word Christian originally meant *like Christ*, not merely a believer in Christ. I remember at a meeting; I once heard a preacher say that believing in Christ means nothing because even the devil himself believes in Christ. I am paraphrasing but it is close enough to carry the same punch. If your belief does not make you more like Christ, you are believing something other than what Christ taught in word and deed,

I worked in the cafeteria for much of my undergraduate college experience. It was a heinous, disgusting experience to work in the dishwashing room, scraping uneaten food and draining chewing tobacco spittle into a trough that led to a massive garbage disposal. The room was filled with loud, steamy equipment, a room-sized dishwasher that took specialized sections of the brain to load and unload as a conveyor belt moved dishes non-stop. The din of the dishwasher, disposal, the clanging of silverware being sorted, and the music being played over a loudspeaker was deafening.

One day a girl who was a star at feeding dishes into the dishwasher, approached me after our shift as I stood at the timeclock, ready to punch out. She was in a bad mood. As she impatiently elbowed me out of her way to punch out, "What is it with you? You're always so fucking happy. Why don't you ever frown, even just once?"

I tried but it made me laugh.

"You are not normal." She shouted walking away. "Have a bad day!"

I was in shock. Liam was in stitches.

To be honest, I had had a lot of bad days, especially in that room. If it were not for the comradery of others, like Liam and a few more, I would have been a miserable cur. I suppose she had not noticed, or perhaps no matter how bad my day was going, she always thought I was doing better than she. I punched out, and Liam and I went and ate lunch.

That evening in small group Bible study, I told my brothers about the event. They all agreed that I could have and should have used the moment to witness to her. They gave me quippy things to say, offered me tracts to give her or suggested I invite her to fellowship. I never did. She did not seem to like me, and I thought inviting her to fellowship might actually prove counterproductive.

I wanted to be better at witnessing. There were many times early in my Christian walk when I did not speak up even if I had the words. I was not really afraid of what would happen. I simply did not want to mess up. On the occasions that I had forced myself to say something, it had fallen on deaf ears, or garnered a dirty look or comment.

I got better at it and witnessed to the point of being obnoxious. I gave my testimony at every opportunity. I already have mentioned trying to dissuade students from kegger parties and standing in Time Square with a microphone. I passed out tracts, inviting people to fellowship and offering to pray with them. I produced and posted signs all over campus and I even wrote a personal testimonial tract and distributed it. Later in New York City, I approached people on the subway, sat down with folks in public parks. I talked to businesspeople, drug addicts, homeless people and just anyone who would listen. There was a time and place to do that sort of thing but through it all, I understood the lesson I learned that day at the timeclock.

One day, as I was beginning a study in the book of Acts, I noticed the word *be* in Acts 1:8. The word glowed on the page. Witnessing was an act of being not necessarily doing something specific. My job was to be me and be ready. That was all.

You have to first *be* a witness. The evidence of your faith is in who you are, not in an image you present to the world, even in the things you say or do not say. Anyone can fake an image. They are called "wolves in sheep's clothing" (Matthew 7:15). It does not matter if others do not fully understand the reason you are the way you are. It is OK if they just think you are nice, happy, or pleasant. You have to be a human, a real person with something that others want for themselves. The Holy Spirit does not *need* you. Someone else is not going to suffer eternal fire if you do not speak up. That is just silly. It is the credibility of your life that lends weight to your example. And sometimes, the way you handle your won frailty, your mistakes, your failures, speaks louder than anything you might say.

Let's get back to my point. Your belief changes you. Or better said, your belief causes you to think and behave accordingly. You will live according to your belief, no matter what, even if you do not have the words to explain exactly what you believe. So, take the time to understand what you do believe. Do not worry about getting it right nor exact. It is going to change anyway.

In my professional practice today, I help many people discover and work out their core values while managing their inner conflict and their own natural inconsistencies. When I am working with someone with religious trauma, my clients are sometimes surprised when we start talking about what they believe. They are even more surprised when they try to answer by telling me what they no longer believe, and I insist that they have not really answered the question.

"Ok, now that we know what you don't believe, what do you believe?"

"Nothing," they might say.

"That's impossible," I might say and then explain the nature and purpose of memory and how the unconscious mind works.

Ultimately, we are working toward a renewed sense of trusting ourselves and our own judgment.

As in the case of any trauma, minor or severe, religious or otherwise, we have to deal directly with and process the trauma. Trauma is like a scratch on the brain. In the days of vinyl records, the needle would get stuck on a scratched record and repeat a short bit of song over and over again. A severe scratch might cause the needle to skip and play only disjointed parts of the song. Traumatic scratches on the mind do the same thing. We might relive a traumatic event over and over, rekindling the emotions and the reactions we had at the time, sometimes compounding our trauma. We may ruminate on the thoughts, the memories, the things we should have or should not have said or done.

Traumatic scratches can be repaired but it takes work, time, and mental processing to heal and frankly the scratch may leave a scar with which one must live. You can move beyond your trauma, no matter what the initial cause.

Chapter 11

Wat Yannawa and the Final Challenge

I was offered a prostitute within an hour of arriving at Bangkok Airport. I chose to go to Thailand mostly because of the cost and the food. It was spring break at the university and most of the faculty were traveling. I would have stayed at home except for a fair portion of my paycheck each month went to paying to heat my apartment. I paid more in gas and electricity bills for my tiny efficiency apartment in Japan than I had spent in rent in New York City.

It was cheaper for me to fly to Thailand, stay in a hotel, and eat in restaurants for nearly three weeks, than for me to pay for the utilities in my apartment in Hiroshima.

As for the food, the flavors of Japanese cuisine are distinctly subtle. My palate in Japan was limited by what I could afford and what was available in the grocery store. Before leaving the States, it had not occurred to me to bring things like spices with me. I like Japanese food but was truly hungry for flavor. Thai food is wonderfully flavorful.

At the customs desk in Bangkok Airport, the officer asked me why I wanted such a long visa. I was asking for nearly a month to cover the event of a canceled flight. "I live in Japan," I said. "I'm hungry."

One of several guards translated what I said for the benefit of the others. They all laughed, stamped my passport and I went through customs without a hitch.

My hotel, cheap by American standards, was near a district of the city known for night life. That also meant that some clubs pandered sex workers. I knew it. I was curious about the attitudes regarding paid sexual encounters but not about the sex itself. After all, AIDS was a major concern at the time, and I did not want to bring back HIV as a souvenir of an encounter with a prostitute. Also, my ethic was that sex had to come from mutual, not paid desire.

Danilo was fading from my life. Our correspondence had grown sparse with not much to say. He was dating someone else and he encouraged me to do the same. I was not really inclined toward casual sex though I do not know what I would have done if I had met someone with whom I shared mutual attraction and no financial remuneration.

By that time, I had come to terms with the idea that other people were more than comfortable with my being gay. The first semester I was in Japan, another professor, whose name I no longer remember, invited me to dinner. I do not know how he knew of my struggle as I had kept it to myself, but at the dinner, we spoke frankly about my sexuality and my faith and the difficulty I had in reconciling the two.

He was patient and listened. He did, however, mention something that rang the bell of memory harkening back to my last sermon at the church in the Bronx. "You have to know yourself," he counseled. "But not only know yourself, but you also need to accept and respect yourself. It's not easy being gay in the world in which we live. If you do not love yourself, no one else really can love you. If you do not respect yourself, no one else ever will." That was human advice without reference to God or the scriptures, but it pierced my heart all the same. I knew he was right. It was what I had preached about in the last sermon.

I am not sure how it happened. Gradually, among the faculty and staff it was assumed that I was gay. By the middle of the second semester, by the time I went to Thailand, I had opened my mind to the possibility of meeting someone like Danilo with whom I could explore a longer term, perhaps permanent relationship. Given the shortness of stay in Japan, much less Thailand, such a possibility would require nothing short of a miraculous convergence of events and circumstances.

The lobby of the hotel was adequately decorative, but no one stayed at that hotel for the decor. The cab driver carried my bag to the front desk and handed it off to one of the bellmen standing nearby. I checked in, and in my room, as the bellman set my suitcase on the stand, he asked,

"Can I help you find a girl?"

"No thank you." I was still prudish enough to be shocked.

"A boy maybe?"

"No thank you," I chuckled, noticeably nervous.

93

"How about me?" he smiled.

I thanked him for the offer with a generous tip and some inane response about being tired from the trip. My heart was beating hard as I locked the door behind him. The conversation was too frank, too up-front and made me wonder if I had indeed chosen a good hotel. As I said, the hotel was near nightlife, but it was supposedly not in the red-light district.

Now let me be a bit more transparent. I was tempted. Let's face reality. I was a thirty-year-old man who could count his sexual partners on a single hand with fingers left over. I was alone in a foreign country in which the sex trade was apparently a normal thing. There was no one to judge me but myself. Clearly to the bellman, who was younger and fitter than I was and who had probably done the same thing a thousand times, the encounter would have meant next to nothing but some cash. Yes, I was tempted.

I have to admit that I have always been a sort of rebel when it came to certain aspects of sexual conduct prescribed in the Christian communities to which I ascribed. There is a Bible verse that suggests that if someone is horny, they should get married (1 Corinthians 7:9). Now there is a marriage made in heaven, right? Being horny is a great reason to marry someone, especially for teenage boys who are nearly constantly so. There is a reason many young men carry their schoolbooks at the side of their hips and not cradled in their arms. The books provide convenient cover in case a part of them inexplicably springs to life. It happens all the time in puberty. Being horny is part of being an adolescent.

I bring up this verse because in our modern context if taken literally, the verse is not only inappropriate, but also downright dangerous. At the time the book was written, the life expectancy was shorter, marriages were commonly arranged, and people, especially girls, married early.

Perhaps if sex were not such a taboo subject in the church, we might have healthy discussions that could help young people practically and realistically navigate the changes in their bodies. Instead, we lay down rules and offer them moral platitudes hoping that as responsible young Christians, they will not act on their urges.

The notion that God is offended by masturbation has always troubled me. The world is filled with ugliness, crimes, murders, rapes, and cruelty yet, an almighty, all-knowing, omnipresent God is upset and offended by some kid pleasing himself in the shower? Are we really supposed to believe that?

The rationale that converted masturbation from natural to sinful simply never made sense to me. Leaders explained that masturbation was wrong because it was the "unrighteous satisfying of a righteous desire." Meaning sexual desire was "righteous," but only in the context of marriage.

The vocalist Jessica Simpson lost a career in Christian music because her breasts were considered too distracting for young Christian men. Just imagine being told you could not sing in church because your breasts were too big and you might inspire boys in the congregation to go home and masturbate.

I was once engaged in a conversation with a fundamentalist man who insisted that sexual activity was created only for the purposes of procreation. I asked, "Shall we inform your wife that the only reason you approach her sexually is to have another child? Do you think she would like hearing that, lie though it may be?"

Masturbation does not hurt anyone. In fact, it is a fair and reasonable remedy for being horny, especially during sexual development. Granted, it could become a problem if a young person is constantly masturbating, but most people do not take it that far.

One summer, I shared an apartment with a fellowship brother because his apartment was close to the mall where I had a summer job. One day he confessed his problem.

"I guess you know that I struggle with masturbation," he said from his bed buried under a comforter. He must have thought I had caught him in the act. The statement took me by surprise. I told him I had not noticed, hoping that would be the end of an uncomfortable conversation. Even then, I personally did not think masturbation was terribly wrong, and I did not really care whether he masturbated or not as long as I was not a constant witness to it.

One day, shortly thereafter, as I walked into the apartment, I was overwhelmed by the smell of airplane glue. I could hardly breathe. There was my roommate sitting at the dining room table, putting together a plastic model car. "What are you doing?" I asked, referring to the smell throwing open the windows. "You're going to get really high, or you are going to pass out!"

"I went to see my pastor. He told me that I could avoid masturbating if I got a hobby."

My eyes still roll in my head when I think about that stupid advice. Apart from getting high on the glue, I could not and still cannot see how putting together a plastic model car could substitute for masturbation.

If my addressing this issue makes you uncomfortable, you need to not only wake up and smell the coffee, but you also need to drink a strong cup or two. Sex, even among unmarried Christians, is not unheard of. I stand by my assessment. If we were not so prudish about sex and we could discuss it a bit more honestly, and frankly, young people would have a healthier understanding of sex and its role in their lives.

They call Thailand the land of smiles and that bellman smiled at me every time I walked through the lobby. I did not go to night clubs by myself. I had thought I would, but I really enjoyed walking around the streets illuminated by strands of lightbulbs wrapping vendor booths that sold everything from pirated CDs to textiles. It was a bit cooler in the evening and the displays reminded me of summer festivals.

One evening I went to a restaurant that had a telephone on each table. When my phone rang, I thought it had to be a joke. "Are you alone or waiting for someone else?" the voice asked.

I wondered if this was another proposition. "I'm alone."

"You don't have to eat alone. Look to your left. I'll wave. Please feel free to join my friend and me for dinner." I looked, saw a casually dressed man with dark brown hair and a visible five o'clock shadow that reminded me of Fred Flintstone. His friend was younger, blond, and looked well-scrubbed.

Jim and Barry were from Canada. They were a gay couple who had come to see the sights and taste the flavors of Thailand. They seemed amused by the sex club scene.

They were really quite nice. We spent an afternoon sightseeing and a couple of evenings together for dinner and a club afterward. The first club was a disco that seemed much like Mickey's except when the show started, it had nothing much to do with dancing. I was too far away to know if the actors were actually doing what it looked like. Jim assured me they were doing exactly what it looked like.

On another evening we went to a different club, more like a bar. This one was just an excuse for prostitution. Young men wearing numbered buttons milled about the crowd, flirting, drinking, and being playful. The protocol was to pick one that you liked, pay the bar for their absence, and take them away for your pleasure at a price you negotiated. This information was offered to me by a total stranger, I suppose, in response to my troubled expression and obvious discomfort.

One evening, after Jim and Barry had gone to a beach resort in Phuket, I ventured out alone. I found one of the bars that they had pointed out and went in alone. I sat at the bar, nursing a drink (I have never been much for alcoholic beverages) when I was approached by a young man in his early twenties. He wore a numbered badge and showed me his English Language School ID card.

I thought to myself, *here is an opportunity to learn something. Maybe he speaks enough English to answer my questions.* I paid the bar the prostitute fee. I also paid for a disgustingly filthy room above the bar, and there we went. There was a disheveled sheet on a stained mattress and a used condom in the ashtray. I found the cleanest place I could to sit down and we began to talk.

I asked him perhaps too many questions that were too personal and none of my business, but he was polite and answered most of them. He told me a number of interesting things.

The owner of the bar was very protective of him and the other boys. They did not have to go with anyone they did not like, and there were guards, lots of them, should they need help. He said he was lucky to be working in that bar.

He was collecting gold chains from patrons, and that was his way of saving for retirement. He also hoped to meet a rich man who would take care of him for the rest of his life but all of his friends who had once boarded that gravy train had been sent back to Thailand within a year. That is why he was saving up the gold. He was not always attracted to the men who paid him for sex, but it was over soon enough, and he earned more money than he needed. Whenever he had enough extra, he would buy gold.

The only question he had for me was why I did not want to have sex with him. I guess he thought I would not pay him unless we did the deed but paying for sex was not in my psychological purview. I explained I was just interested in understanding more about people. He accepted my explanation as well as my cash.

That sums up my experiences in Thailand, except for my third challenge which came with a shaved head and swathed in a saffron-colored robe.

Thailand in April is exceedingly hot and humid. I was and am a walker of neighborhoods. I do not like to plan too much. I like to have an idea of where I would like to end up, but I do not focus on the destination. For me, it is not about getting there but whatever I notice or find along the way. If I do not get where I wanted to go, I can try again tomorrow. As a consequence, I have, more than once, very nearly gotten into serious trouble.

I had a list of several *must-see* sites and had circled them on a map of the city. Every day, I would set out and explore my way to a different destination. On one day, my journey included a ferry across the river. On the way back, I sat next to a saffron-robed monk who was likely my age but looked a lot younger. He struck up a simple conversation with me and as the ferry docked, he invited me to visit his temple, enticing me explaining that Wat Yannawa, was incredibly famous. The temple looked like a boat.

Thailand is full of Buddhist temples and I had seen many of them, and if I am honest, enough of them. This was an opportunity to see one from the inside out at the invitation of a smiling monk. For the first time, I would not perhaps feel like an intruder or an intrepid but skeptical explorer.

We never entered the temple proper, but he led me beyond a decaying cement wall to his lodgings. The monks' lodgings were simple cement structures mostly open to the environment, noticeably cooler inside. There was no furniture. The floors were swept and clean. Outside in the courtyard of the Temple, children were laughing and playing. I imagined they were orphans because my missionary heart had dreamed of caring for orphans, but I do not know. It may well have been a daycare or a school.

We spent several companionable hours talking. I do not remember exactly what we spoke about, but I do remember being mentally engaged in an ethical or moral discovery process. I was comparing the ethics and morals expressed by the monk with my own.

Apart from the Japanese people I had met from the town where I lived, I had only known a few Buddhists in my life, all of them Americans who had grown disillusioned with western faiths. One, another professor in Japan, was so tightly wound, he was the very anthesis of the monk. Desire and attachment are seen as significant causes of suffering in Buddhism, and yet, my colleague chanted because he wanted the universe to give him the objects of his desire, the way many Christians pray. He seemed to believe that by chanting, he could influence the universe to give him what he wanted. On one occasion I asked him if chanting for what he wanted was not the opposite of what he should be doing. Should he not be chanting to be free of desire. My question frustrated him and we never spoke of it again.

Early in my life, when I was still a practicing Catholic, I had read a book comparing Buddhism and Catholicism. Although I considered Buddhism as idolatry, while at the same time, not disparaging the statues in a Roman Catholic church, my biggest mental argument against Buddhism was that it was not Christian. Now it must be stated that there are lots of kinds of Buddhists in the world. There is a real and practical difference between Thai Buddhism, Tibetan Buddhism and the type of Buddhism practiced in Japan.

When it was time for me to go back to my hotel, the good monk walked me to the temple gate and extracted a promise from me to return the next day. My time in Thailand was nearing an end. I had honestly had enough of walking the streets of Bangkok. They were dirty, smoggy, and seething with heat and humidity. Going and meeting this new friend and talking was a delightful way of spending my last few days.

Sometimes other monks joined our discussions. I suppose I was as much a novelty for them as they were for me, and as I left the temple grounds for the last time, I confronted the final challenge to the structure of my faith.

On the way back to my hotel, my mind was filled with the events of the last few days, my time with the Buddhist monk. All that remained of the nightlife was a kind of ethnocentric sadness that people had to make their living having sex with strangers, especially in a time when AIDS was so prevalent and frightening.

It occurred to me that ethically and morally, my monk friend had demonstrated more Christian ideals and behaviors in a matter of a few days than most Christians had in years. He did not profess Christianity, but he exemplified many of the traits that I saw as Christ-like. I was confronted by the essential claim that one had to be a Christian to be like Christ Was it better to be a Christian who was not much like Christ or hold some other doctrine that actually brought about a practical expression that I characterized as *Christian?*

I am aware of the scriptures which say that believing in Jesus is the most important thing and Acts 4:12 is among the most direct. I am also aware of the history of the Bible, the point of view of the authors, and the theological preference therein expressed. When Jesus declared himself to be the way, the truth, and the life, what exactly was he saying? Was he saying we must live under the umbrella of his name, or we must become like him? (John 14)

If confessing Christ did not universally have the effect of causing believers to become more like Christ, what was the value of the declaration? One knows a tree by the fruit it produces. That was the teaching of Jesus himself. If that man had not been wearing a saffron-colored robe, I would have sworn the man was a Christian. In fact, one of the most Christian people I had ever met.

If you are reading this book to look for reasons why I should be denounced as a heretic, I have already given you plenty of evidence. Have at it if you must, but if you are reading this because you struggle with some of the things you have been taught as a Christian, I humbly ask you to wait until the end of the book. We are almost there.

The following summer, I spent a month in New York. I sublet a small apartment in Chelsea. I still had not yet entirely decided that I would lead a gay owned and operated life. I still hung precariously between gay owned and operated and a celibate life as a minister of the gospel. At the time, I had no way of meshing the two.

I visited the church in the Bronx and was warmly received. I visited old friends, met their new baby, visited even older friends, and tooled around the city as kind of a final farewell. I knew I would not return to that city to live anymore. After another year commitment to the university in Hiroshima, I would resettle in sunny Los Angeles. I was already contemplating pursuing a PhD at the University of Southern California.

Chapter 12

I Like Your Hat

When I moved back to Angeles, two hopes I had for my life were dashed. I did not get the job I wanted at Santa Monica College and I did not get into the graduate program at USC. Believe it or not, it was the first time I did not get a job I wanted and the first time I had been rejected by a school. The result was that my life was wide open.

I attended my first gay pride parade and festival within days of my arrival in the city. That morning, we had had a fairly strong earthquake tremor that had shaken me up a bit, so I was already a little on edge. The sun was hot and beat on my bald scalp. I used a gay rag newspaper called *Frontiers* to make a hat to shield myself from the sun.

There were literally thousands of people lined up along Santa Monica boulevard waiting for the parade to start. In the distance, I could hear the roar of motorcycles and in moments a group known as Dykes on Bikes were revving their engines and weaving patterns in front of us. I cannot explain why, but I started to cry.

Group after group marched by to the roaring cheers and applause of the crowd. I had never seen so many gay people in one place, much less seen any gay person actually celebrating who they were. I confess I cried throughout the parade. Waves of emotion cleansed me of my fears, comforted me for the pain I had suffered, and seeded joy in my heart. People gave me tissues, asked me if I was alright, total strangers sat next to me on the ground and put their arms around me in comfort.

One of the groups that marched by was AIDS Project Los Angeles (APLA). My heart melted. In the Christian community, a number of vocal preachers had declared AIDS the judgment of God on sinful people. From the first time I heard it, it sounded ridiculously stupid like when the same preachers declare that a natural disaster happened because God was upset over a recent change of law or social tolerance for sin.

As the group approached, all the people on either side stood up, applauded, and cheered. A standing ovation for a group of people who had dedicated themselves to helping people with AIDS. In my mind, I remember thinking about the song "When the Saints Go Marching In." As I stood up for them, thanking them, cheering them on, I knew I belonged with them. I wanted to be in their number. I volunteered as soon as I found a job in LA, and it was three years before I was hired to put together the Living Skills Program.

Finally came the grand marshals of the parade, Dick Seargent and Elizabeth Montgomery. Their car stopped right in front of me. I am not usually a star-struck person, but it had been a very emotional couple of hours. Elizabeth Montgomery leaned out of the car and spoke directly to me. "Honey, I love your hat! So chic and practical, too!" I was speechless.

In Matthew Chapter 9, Jesus is eating dinner at Matthew's house and lots of the guests were labeled as sinners by the Pharisees. They questioned Jesus' association with them. Jesus' retort was simple. The sick, not the healthy, needed a doctor.

I had always read that verse thinking Jesus was hanging out with the sinners to convert them, to save them, to redeem them. That same argument had been one that I presented to my house brothers the day I was confronted by the judgment committee. I tried to get them to see that it was acceptable for me to go and hear Liam play as part of my witness. I did not drink. I had not even stayed through an entire song.

It had been a hollow argument falling on deaf ears. The honest truth was that I went to hear Liam play because it was important to Liam and I valued him and his friendship. And they pushed me to make a choice between him and them making the decision equal to my choosing Liam or Jesus.

When Jesus spoke to the criticism of the Pharisees, He was not suggesting that the Pharisees were not sick and did not need him. The people at the party knew there was room for improvement in their lives. The Pharisees were too blindly hypocritical and self-righteous to know that they needed him too. There was no significant difference between the Pharisees and the so-called sinners at the party except that the Pharisees were too egotistical to see it. (Matthew 23:27)

Although for perhaps another year, I harbored the idea of a meeting with the folks at Church on the Way, it was a private, nostalgic notion. Even then, I knew that I could not go back to that old way of thinking, not practically, and definitely not spiritually. If I dared open my mouth to explain any of the past two years, I would most likely be asked to leave. I would forever more be a kind of outcast in that religious world. I would have to completely fake it to make it there and well, I am no hypocrite.

I remember my interview for the position at APLA. I had been volunteering in the Buddy program for three years. A buddy was a kind of assigned friend for a client of the agency. I also became a Buddy support group facilitator for groups of buddies to meet and provide mutual support.

In volunteering at APLA, I had two buddies in three years. I met with my first buddy always in a public place. We never discussed AIDS, how he was feeling or anything medical. He had told me at our first meeting that he had enough friends expressing concern over the progression of his disease. He did not need another one, but he wanted to just be a human; someone with whom AIDS was no longer the central theme of the relationship.

I easily obliged. He was personable enough and I know how to hold up my half of a conversation.

My second buddy needed a chauffeur, which was not part of the description of the volunteer position, but I did not mind. I would pick him up outside his building, and we would run errands. I would take him to doctor's appointments or help him carry groceries to his apartment. Sometimes we would share a meal. Of course, we talked the whole time. He was a chatty guy from Arkansas who seemed bent on impressing me. I would not have chosen him as a friend because we were simply different. I was older and more stable. He was younger and just a bit silly. I think the best word to describe my relationship with him is avuncular. To him, I was a kind, patient, even indulgent uncle.

It was in training for the Buddy program that I learned how to spot and gently call out manipulative behavior. Lots of people can be manipulative. In nicer circles, it might be called persuasion, but there are lots of techniques that people use to get others to do what they want. Simple quid pro quo is the most obvious, but talented manipulators have lots of tricks and usually get what they want.

Manipulation is common in churches. I saw this demonstrated in the most recent church I attended regularly for a while. I saw it on the part of the pastor, an assistant pastor, and most obviously in someone deemed by a major Pentecostal denomination to be a recognized prophet. Sometimes it is quite subtle: "I have a vision for God's ministry for this church. Will you be a part of it? Pray about it. I believe that God is doing [X, Y or Z]." For most people who do not have the foggiest idea about what God is doing and trust the pastor, these phrases alone can be quite powerful and manipulative.

A number of years ago, I reconnected with some people from my old college fellowship. I had been missing a church family and hoped in the intervening years that some congregations might have become more comfortable with gay people. My husband and I began attending a local Assembly of God congregation.

An old friend and I were seated in the church. The so-called prophet was introduced to the congregation. The first people to receive one of his prophecies was the assistant pastor in charge of the service that evening and his wife. They were called forward and with bowed heads and joyful hearts, they heard "the word of the Lord." If it was to be believed, God gave them a very favorable review. Five stars!

"I have seen your heart and am working mightily in your life [blah. . . blah]." After that, the prophet could proceed to do whatever he wanted with impunity. If that pastor did anything to discredit the shenanigans of that so-called prophet, he would be invalidating that favorable performance review that supposedly came from God for both himself and his wife.

What I witnessed after that was nothing more than a cheap, cold-reading show of an experienced "psychic" charlatan. At one point, he picked out a young couple in the audience and asked them to stand up. They did. "Are you married?"

"No."

"How long have you been dating?" he asked.

"Two years."

Then looking at the young man, "Don't you think it is time you popped the question?" The young man bowed his head but did not respond.

I was appalled, and I whispered something along those lines to my friend. It may be reasonable to assume that two people who have been dating for two years are getting along and might marry, but this was tantamount to telling them God wanted them to marry. That truly crossed a line.

"And you were involved in the occult!" he addressed the young woman. He proceeded to tell her that remnants of the occult remained in her life but that God would cleanse her of them. Her head fell, and she began to weep.

My friend, who bought the show hook, line, and sinker, leaned into me. "There," she whispered. "How would he know that? He's real!"

I rolled my eyes, "Perhaps by the pentagram tattooed on her arm. I noticed it when we were walking through the lobby. She was not covering it up!" I shot back. "I'll bet she has to hock something to get that tattoo removed."

My friend saw me as unreasonably skeptical, but I looked up the prophet later online and discovered that he charged $1,500 for a private prophecy session, as if anyone could get God to speak for a price (Acts 8:18-23). I never went back to that church.

I had to take a fifty percent cut in pay to take the job of Living Skills Coordinator at APLA. The plans they had for the Living Skills Program were ambitious, much of which was never realized. We never, for example, created a laundry for clients to wash their clothes. There were no nap rooms for people to nap. We never created the hair salon/barber shop they had planned. But even without such things, the program became something special.

They gave me an office out of which I was to run the program, which was to provide social, educational, and recreational activities as well as some direct services to people living with symptomatic HIV infection. Within a week, the volunteer office began sending me all the potential volunteers they thought would be useful. (These were mostly people they did not know how to use otherwise.) They sent me yoga instructors, a chiropractor, two volunteer clinical hypnotists, dance instructors, astrologists, make-up artists, a piano teacher, and a bunch of people who did not fit or did not want to fit in other programs.

My first real volunteer was a guy named Luke who offered his administrative skills. He had known about the program and had been waiting for them to hire someone to fill the job. I met him on my first day when he popped into the office to tell me he wanted to volunteer. He was there almost as soon as I was, and he never left.

The building was an old Hollywood production studio. The program organically grew so fast that within a few months we were building out a large studio space as the Living Skills Center. Once I had developed a participation tracking program, I documented that we had more than 2000 clients actively participating in one or more activities each month, many participating several times a week. The program became internationally recognized as the best in class and AIDS service organizations from as far away as Thailand called or visited our center for information and details on developing a program of their own.

It was at once the hardest and most rewarding job I have ever had. Luke, all the volunteers, and I worked tirelessly. Apart from coordinating the program, my job was a cross between Mother Teresa and a cruise director on a ship. I spent my day organizing, hugging, meeting, scheduling, and handing out snacks.

I met and talked to every client that participated in our program. I was granted the grace to see the beloved child of God in every one of them. I did not talk much about my faith in that place. It would have been inappropriate.

Most of my clients were gay men. Christians have not been nice to gay people in general. And many members of the church have been distinctly cruel, priggish, and unloving. As a result, in gay circles, expressing Christian faith can raise barriers of anger and resentment for past religious traumas wrought by Christians.

I kept a candy dish on my desk for clients to nibble as we talked. One sweet guy named Teddy would visit every few days. He particularly liked the Mary Jane candies, a kind of individually wrapped peanut butter chew that I got in bags. One day, as Teddy rummaged through the bowl of candies, he discovered the Mary Janes were gone. I saw the disappointment in his eyes. I pulled a small handful of them out of my drawer. They were the last of the bag, and I had saved them for Teddy, knowing he might visit before I could buy more.

He actually teared up a bit. I expect it was because he understood that I had thought of him, not as a client but as a person. After he left my office, I swear I heard God speak to my heart. "If you had remained as you were, I could not have used you here." I closed my door, wept and thanked God for his loving-kindness toward me and thanked him for allowing me to be part of his care for our clients.

Joseph A. Onesta

Chapter 13

Going Public

For decades, the Catholic church has been dealing with sex abuse charges leveled against clergy for perpetrating the abuse and against the denomination for attempting to cover up the scandal and not properly addressing the issue. The furor eventually died back and fell into the hands of ambulance-chasing attorneys who wanted their financial share of the trauma of the victims.

It must be said that these scandals are not the unique domain of the Catholic Church. Emotional, sexual, and physical abuse happens in virtually every context in which some individuals are perceived in spiritual authority over others. The abuse is perpetrated on children and adults, males and females of every conceivable creed, ethnicity, or race.

Victims of this abuse in religious contexts, rarely speak out for a variety of reasons that outsiders find difficult to understand.

First, and I think foremost, is the essential belief in the religion itself that causes the victim to perhaps not recognize or even feel responsible for the abuse. That is, the victim sees the abuse as a natural consequence of their belief or of their gullibility. At first, they do not see it as abuse. They may view the perpetrator(s) as having their best interest at heart and only later come to regard it as abuse.

The second most common reason seems to be an acquired sense of having *deserved* the abuse. It may have been presented as a positive thing as in, "You are very special to me." Other times, the abuse is presented as an antidote for some misbehavior or aberrant act. The latter, when dolled out as punishment or correction, often happens in full view, approval and even participation of the congregation. Keep in mind that in that case, the congregation is being both used and abused at the same time because while they are party to the discipline, no matter how severe, they are also being warned that the same thing could happen to them if they misbehave.

Lastly but still very pervasive is that victims may suffer a sense of shame about what they have experienced. Shame is vastly different from guilt. A guilty person may wonder why they allowed themselves to be part to an event. A person who feels ashamed not only feels culpable but responsible for the event. It may be that the event itself has sullied or irrevocably stained them in some way.

In my practice as a hypnotherapist, I once welcomed a husband and wife who were having difficulties with intimacy and trust. Usually, I would refer this sort of problem to a licensed marriage and family therapist, but this couple had been to see several and were exploring the option of hypnosis as a way of working through their difficulties.

The source of the discomfort with intimacy was eventually revealed. The wife, who knew her husband to be a kind and trustworthy man, had previously suffered a major traumatic abuse. In her younger days, she had rebelled against the Evangelical rules in her family and led a rather reckless life, frequently drinking, occasionally using drugs and having sex whenever and with whomever she wanted.

One evening she met am attractive, personable man in a bar and accepted an invitation to his home. The home, a trailer several miles down a dirt road in the Arizona desert, became her prison for over a year. She had been beaten and sometimes starved. For months, she was chained to fixtures in the bathroom. Eventually, her captor removed the chains. She remained in the trailer alone while he went off to work his construction jobs. I asked her to describe her motivations for staying when she knew he would be gone all day.

"I always imagined him coming back early and catching me." That was the practical reason, but there was more. She explained that two things were happening in her mind. She thought she was being punished by God, that she was reaping what she had sown.

Any rational person knows that she had certainly taken a risk by going home with a stranger. Any rational person should also acknowledge that she did not deserve what she experienced.

Her past experiences and perceptions had trained her to *believe* that the risk of sleeping with a stranger was worth taking, that it probably was no risk at all. She had done the same thing many times without much problem. This time, events took a different course, and she was traumatized by them. That traumatic experience left her unable to trust her own judgment, particularly about men. Though she intellectually knew her husband was nothing like her abuser, her trauma taught her to be suspicious of her own estimation of him.

Religion played a role in her trauma because she believed that God was punishing her for rejecting the rigid Evangelical Christianity of her parents. She thought that she somehow had *earned* the trauma. Despite her being averse to saying so, in her mind, the abuse was her fault. The very thought is irrational.

She took a risk, and because her past experiences minimized the risk in her mind, she was vulnerable and became a victim. That is what it was. She was operating on a belief. We always operate on a belief even when we do not recognize the belief or cannot vocalize it.

Telling her story to others presented an even greater risk for re-traumatization. Heaping trauma on top of trauma, her parents, though aghast at what happened to their daughter, believed what happened to her was a result of her rebelling against God and felt compelled to point it out, possibly to preclude her doing it again or to get her back into the church. My client was again traumatized when her perceptions about punishment were confirmed by her parents.

I also point out that her experience in a way, traumatized her parents. Most victims of religious trauma resent my pointing out that the trauma spreads to the people around them as well; sometimes to the very people they may see as having caused their trauma. But trauma, like a virus can spread. Remember my friend who told me of his misgivings at our pastor's offer of a special friendship? For me, the trauma was minor, one that I could simply explain away. I did not have to look at it, consider it or even think about a response. However, he had to deal with the fear, insecurity and with the pastor on his own.

Being gay was never a choice for me. I grew up in a time when homosexuality was still seen as a mental illness. Based on the attitudes around me, I was convinced that there was something wrong with me. Constant bullying caused my formative years to be spent in survival mode. There was a long period of time in which I believed that I deserved everything I experienced.

Thus, when I heard that God had made other gay people straight, I considered it a matter of course. Why God was waiting to send that same miracle my way was nothing short of frustrating. So, when I hear the argument that gay people have chosen that lifestyle, I point out that I long chose to not be gay but, in the end, sexuality is not a matter of choice.

When I eventually revealed my acceptance of living a gay owned and operated life to some of my dearest and closest friends and family, I received a lot of support from my family and some support from my church friends, but most of them found my decision to be unacceptable and I lost their presence in my life, a presence I highly valued at the time. The loss was another trauma in the name of religion.

When I am working with clients, coping with the reactions of friends and family is perhaps the most emotionally conflicted part of the process.

While it is natural for me to focus on my own trauma, my experience in working with victims of trauma informs me that the people I decided to tell may have experienced a bit of trauma of their own and that some of the more dramatic responses on their part were possibly more about their discomfort than mine. I do not blame myself for that. Instead, I blame the systematic and ingrained prejudice and hypocrisy that is constantly reinforced in a socio-religious environment in which people are required to wear masks to be acceptable.

Indeed, I imagine that some readers of this book find its contents disturbing enough to call it traumatizing. Others might well call it liberating.

I have had a number of distraught parents consult with me about using hypnosis as a form of conversion therapy to help their teenager to become straight. Such parents need my attention as much as they think their children do. They are often in turmoil over what they perceive as the fate of their children as well as the social consequences they might face in church by having gay children. They suffer their own anxiety and that angst spills over into their family interactions just making it all worse. It is often the turmoil brought about by the conflict that causes some parents to dismiss their children from the home, incredible though it may be.

In New York, I once attended a group called Life Ministries. The group specifically catered to "ex-homosexuals" or people who wanted to be. I knew several regular members of that group. Each one fit neatly into one of several categories, each categorically nullifying the notion of a gay to straight conversion miracle.

In more than thirty years of ministry, I have never met anyone who credibly had converted from homosexual to heterosexual. I have met and counseled many gay men who married a woman and had children who either repressed their sexuality much to their frustration and misery or led a double life. I have met men and women who have chosen celibacy to honor God. A majority of them came to terms with masturbation or lived with the associated guilt. Some were actually asexual so being celibate was no sacrifice. I even knew an asexual Catholic priest who came to me wanting to feel sexual temptation so that his vow of celibacy would be more meaningful. I have met bisexual people who have chosen to marry, thus eliminating the less acceptable choice. I have met many people who declare themselves heterosexual *in faith*. In other words, they have chosen to lie.

A professor at the college I attended had been prominent faculty sponsor of a campus ministry. On the testimony of multiple credible witnesses, this this professor had been identified offering and performing oral sex on students in public restrooms. He also rented rooms in his home to attractive college students and was discovered surreptitiously filming or photographing them when they were unclothed.

This same professor was asked by a mutual friend and campus ministry leader to counsel me on my decision and in doing so, he invited me to attend the now defunct Exodus International, an international version of Life Ministries. He also suggested I try reparative therapy.

Reparative therapy itself is mentally, emotionally, and often physically abusive for religious purposes. I have never gone through it myself but know people who have. No doubt, many people voluntarily choose to participate in and subject themselves to this abuse. Others are forced or coerced into it by their families or church families. Religious persuasion is often quite coercive.

In the desert, both my spiritual expression and worship became a very personal and private thing. My understanding and experience of the divine expanded. I learned how to relate to God without trying to evaluate my success or progress. I refused to maintain notions of what was or was not acceptable. I was no longer hoping to be a better Christian or even a better minister. I became convinced that my sincere and honest interaction, prayer, meditation or expression was what God wanted and was what I needed.

After my decision to stop waiting for the miracle of heterosexuality and live the best gay life I could, I had a list to make.

121

Whom to tell? It would not be *everyone*. What would be the point of that?

There were some people who deserved to know. The woman to whom I had been engaged deserved that respect because I had used the church as an excuse for not being even respectably physical with her. Others had endorsed me under the sole banner of my work in the church. They had judged my character without knowing the full story. The senior pastor who had sponsored my ordination already knew. Or at least he said he already knew. Whether or not he was still waiting for a miracle of heterosexuality, I will never know. In the thirty years since I sat in his office taking my leave, he has since died.

I chose after that to tell only a few people. I told the family I lived with because I loved them dearly. Their children call me uncle, and these were both friends and family. The mother of this family used to enjoy introducing me as her brother because our distinct appearance gave the declaration a certain shock value. Her husband was truly my best friend throughout my time in New York City and we remain friends and brothers to this day.

In the summer I spent in Chelsea, I held their third child in my arms. In his adult years, he asked me how his parents and I had maintained our relationship because, in his words, "They are so conservative." Conservative they may be, but the secret of that lasting relationship is simple. It is love, unconditional love.

I contacted a few of the people from the cult I had escaped, both some who stayed and others who had left. The person to whom felt closest rejected me, and we did not speak for more than 20 years. Thankfully, we were able to rebuild the burned bridge before she died of cancer. Others pretended to accept me but did not respond to my future attempts to connect with them. The rest came to recognize the love and the trauma we shared, and we remain in contact until today.

My mother and my childhood best friend had less trouble with my being gay than with my leaving the Roman Catholic Church. My father really struggled until one day I cut off one of his disparaging remarks by explaining that I had tried to change but eventually I had to come to terms with what my life was going to be, and that I intended to go after whatever happiness life might give me. He came to accept my decision and embraced the man I married.

At a reunion of my old college fellowship, some approached me with acceptance, some with tolerance, and a few with a bold confrontation. And some discounted me entirely.

I assert that those who refused to accept my disclosure and move beyond it were actually unable to do so because of their own history of perception-generating memories. I have no idea what their experience might have been, but it must have been significant enough. My roommate, the one who was building model cars in our apartment in replacement for a masturbation habit, had an unexplained anger toward gay people. I never brought it up, but he did, more than once in just a couple of months. At the time I worried that he suspected me. In hindsight, I wonder if he had been abused or even just approached by some man at some point and had suffered trauma as a result.

There were people, who for their own religious reasons, felt that I was going astray. I tried to keep my feelings of offense to myself, but I was not always successful. It occurs to me that they genuinely believed that I was deciding for evil and loved me enough to confront me hoping for a reversal of something they could not understand.

I came to understand that when people say, "Love the sinner, hate the sin," it is a rationalization *for them*, not an accusation for the person they are referring to. They do not know how to otherwise process the information. It is their way of dismissing the issue without really addressing it. Any person who uses the phrase is either an immature or intentionally blind Christian.

When someone discloses something as personal as trauma and its cause or source to another person, they are hoping for one of three things. They may be looking for simple understanding, sympathy. They may well be looking for an apology. Or, they may be hoping for real support and an expression of love.

Disclosure forces a reaction and though we think we know how others will respond; we can never truly step into the shoes of someone else. We have to understand that we are responsible for only half that interaction. We chose to disclose. We might try to be as tactful as possible. Beyond that, the reaction of the person we tell is their responsibility.

I would like to tell you a story about my APLA volunteer named Luke. He was perhaps more committed to the program we were developing than any other volunteer or client. Luke was both volunteer and client.

Luke worked tirelessly for the quality and the success of our program. I was paid a pittance and Luke was paid nothing. He worked every day. He never refused an assignment and made a significant contribution of his own ideas and aspirations for the program. Luke deserves as much if not more acknowledgment for the success of the Living Skills program as I.

On the day Luke did not show up, I assumed he had an appointment that he had forgotten to tell me about. On the third day of his absence, I grew worried and contacted his emergency contact person.

"I haven't seen him," she said. "I have his keys. I'll go over and make sure he's alright." She called me back a little later saying he was not home, but she would keep trying.

When three days became more than a week, my concern became alarm. I went to see a friend who worked in case management to see if there were any notations in Luke's file. This was against the rules, but I did it and though my friend never actually told me where Luke was, I left his desk with the address of a hospice.

I went to look for Luke. I found him in a bed in a ward. He had visibly declined and was clearly fading. Upon seeing me, Luke became angry and said so. "I didn't want anyone to know I was here. I didn't want anyone to see me like this."

Now before you think me heartless and cruel, you need to know that first and foremost, I had come to love Luke as a dear friend. We had worked together daily for more than a year. Also, by that time I had known many people who had died young and in the prime of life. At a certain point during a pandemic, death becomes normal and those that remain, have no choice but to develop coping mechanisms.

After his tirade, I stood by his bed. "Who the fuck do you think you are?" His eyes widened in surprise. "You only own half of our friendship. I own the other half, and I have a right to see you. You don't have the right to check out (die) without giving me the chance to say good-bye to someone I really care about."

He softened. We visited for perhaps ten minutes. I told him that I loved him, that I was hoping for a remission but if we did not get one, that it had been both an honor and a privilege to have known and worked with him. I thanked him for all he had done and tearfully told him he had no idea how much he meant to me. I told him he was already missed, that I would not disclose that I had found him to protect him from what would otherwise be a barrage of visitors. Luke was not a hugger. We shook hands and impulsively I kissed the back of his hand. I needed more than a handshake.

When we make decisions out of our own trauma, we see that trauma from the inside out. Trauma is a sticky matter and as long as and to the degree with which we relive the trauma when we think of it, we strengthen it in our own experience. We effectively fill in the blanks of our memory with more powerful details building up resentment, anger, and frustration, all of which can become bitterness.

Bitterness is poison. It changes us in the worst possible ways. Bitterness removes our joy and creates in us a personality that seems to feed and thrive on more bitterness.

A fair number of my religious trauma clients come for help dealing with bitterness and resentment. They have often become rabid atheists, not believing in anything or alternately believing in nothing and assailing those who do believe in something.

Because they have been harmed, because they trusted untrustworthy people or doctrines or religions, they now have difficulty trusting their own judgment. When we practice the usual excusing, ignoring, or explaining away inconsistencies that just do not seem right in our religious experience, we are subtly telling ourselves that our innate judgment is faulty. Our natural reactions seem oddly inconsistent with what we think should be the truth.

When blind faith eventually starts to disintegrate, victims of religious trauma find themselves running away from something without knowing where they are headed. It is more of a reflex than a reaction, but it is a dangerous one. Remember, we are believing beings. The purpose of memories is to form a pattern in our unconscious mind so that we can adequately predict what might happen in any given situation.

Hypnotherapy is exceptionally useful when conducted by a knowledgeable hypnotist who understands religious trauma. Hypnosis helps the unconscious mind reorder the events and their meanings so that the client is once again able to function normally. The traumatic reaction is designed to prevent the recurrence of the traumatic event but at the cost of self-assurance and confidence sometimes to the point of inability to react. Hypnotherapy helps the client put experiences in perspective and once again learn how to trust their own judgment.

When we experience traumas, including religious traumas, our unconscious minds have been wounded. Those wounds can heal but it takes time and processing to do so and they may leave a scar. The unfortunate thing is that when we simply run away from our trauma, it is like dressing an open wound that will not heal. The only way for that wound to heal is for us to get in touch with and once again trust our own system of perceptions that allow belief. Not necessarily religious beliefs but belief in ourselves and trust in our judgment.

The best way to survive religious trauma is to nurture self-love and acceptance and allow that love to grow and extend to others, even possibly reach those who seemingly do harm. Maintaining a position of love and tolerance for differences inoculates us against the infectious bitterness that can develop and fester over time.

Chapter 14

Pittsburgh Open-Minded Christians

A few years after we moved to Pittsburgh to be closer to my family, I went through a season of depression. There was little left of the vibrant family I had once known. When I left Pittsburgh, my extended family was a whole community of its own. I was the youngest of some fifty first cousins! Most of my childhood family playmates were actually children of my first cousins. I have never tried to count them! There were frequent visits. We often spent Sunday afternoons and holidays together.

By the time I came back, most of my aunts, uncles, and many of my first cousins had already died. Their children, those my age and younger had grown apart. The family that remained had grown distant and disconnected. I left southern California to rejoin a family that no longer existed.

Taking early morning walks helped mitigate the depression. One day, I was walking past a large cathedral-like church that reminded me of Hogwarts, with tall stained-glass windows and vaulted ceilings. I decided to go in. I have always appreciated the quiet and the echoes of even slight sounds in vast empty churches.

Much to my surprise, the church was not empty. An early morning mass was in progress. I inched in and sat in a back pew. The priest had an exceptionally kind manner. His homily was learned and challenging. I enjoyed the service and felt uplifted.

I attended daily mass for several months and as my depression lifted, I attributed the respite at least in part to reconnecting with a church family. I began visiting local churches to see if and where I might fit in. I did this on the q.t. mostly because my husband is Catholic, and he had been greatly hurt by the harsh stances taken by his Evangelical and Pentecostal extended family. I wanted to see if there was a church where I could worship in a Pentecostal way.

At one of the first churches I visited, I was pounced upon by a member of their welcoming committee. She was an odd, fidgety woman. Perhaps I was her first visitor. I wondered if she was hoping for some heavenly points if I let her pray with me. She sat next to me, chatting away, asking all sorts of questions that I found annoying.

"Are you saved?" she asked enthusiastically.

Yes.

How long have you been saved? (A question that always bothered me because I have always been a believer.)

"Since I was nineteen," I said giving her a reference to my Larry Tomczak altar call assuming that was the one she would think valid.

"Have you been baptized?" She reminded me of a car salesperson who desperately needed a commission.

"Twice," I said, slightly baiting her.

"Twice? "Her brow raised.

"Yes, once as a baby and once as an adult."

"Oh," she said with a breath of relief. "Infant baptism doesn't count."

"I don't mean to be rude," I said. "But I came here to worship, not to be interrogated."

She was taken aback, and visibly embarrassed. Thankfully, she went as sat somewhere else. I hope, in her next welcoming committee meeting, someone might coach her a little better. As for the service, it was nothing worth repeating the interrogation for.

Most churches require a new member to sit through a tedious class in faith fundamentals that is usually little more than a clarification of the church's statement of faith though it is often dragged out over weeks. Of course, it works in two ways. In that time, a potential new member learns exactly what the doctrinal position of the church is. I imagine that there have been some people who have walked out of those classes due to theological differences.

More so, however, I think it is a message to potential new members that establishes the boundaries of intolerable dissent. *These are the theological points to which we expect our members to adhere.* This, of course, sets the stage for behavioral conformity. If a person goes beyond these points, he or she is not really one of *us*.

I visited any number of churches within reasonable distance to my home. Only one felt like it could be home. It was a newly forming congregation. Most of the people were quite young and young people are often more accepting and tolerant than older folks. The pastor was a young man of military build and bearing who had been a champion kickboxer before his conversion. I attended that congregation for four or five weeks.

At the last service I attended, I was sitting next to a young couple with an infant child. The service was interrupted by a large, looming, mentally unstable man who started shouting at the woman and calling her all sorts of inappropriate names. He was clearly deranged. He began to move in our direction.

Her husband stood up to defend her and their child. Simultaneously, the pastor signaled to two very muscular men, bouncers of a sort. They escorted the potential attacker out of the church. The husband sat back down, and out of the corner of my eye; I noticed the woman's hand shaking as she caressed the infant in her lap. I just leaned over and whispered,

"Pardon me, but I'd like to say something to you. You have a choice. You can choose to give into your fear and insecurity, or you can realize that nothing happened to you or your child. Your husband would have readily defended you, but he didn't have to. Nothing happened. Do not let this experience be of any consequence in your life."

With a look of gratitude, she visibly relaxed.

The next day, I got a call from the pastor of that church. "I'd like to meet and talk with you. You have some ministry experience, am I right?"

I admitted to it and he asked to meet me for lunch. Our time was amiable but when he found out that I am gay, he asked me not to return to the congregation. I did not go back.

At about that time, my husband worked in the emergency room of the local hospital. One day, one of the ER physicians was inviting people to an event at his church and my husband announced, "Oh, Joseph might be interested in this. He's a minister." I had met the good doctor and his wife, another physician, at the staff holiday party. They were genuinely nice people.

The doctors, of course, knew we were partners. When I learned of the invitation, I wondered if this could possibly be a welcoming church. At their invitation we visited the church and, after the service, joined their family for lunch. It was a lovely visit. I enjoyed the service, the conversation at lunch and their company.

On our second visit to the church, the senior pastor came running to greet us after the service. At the time, I was more than impressed with that attention. Given the size of the congregation and what I imagined to be the staff to manage it, I would have guessed that a visitor welcome would have been delegated to a junior. I cynically suspected that his attention was in response to the prompting of the two successful physicians whose tithes could not have been negligible.

The doctors must have held back at least some information from him because I attracted the attention from one of the junior pastors, who made a point of inviting me to lunch. Neither my husband nor I brandish rainbow flags or wear pink triangles. My conversation with the assistant pastor never got to the point where I felt obliged to point out my sexuality. At that, I still did not know how much the doctors had said about us.

I am guessing, and I admit it is a guess, that the intention of that lunch was a "would he fit in with our staff" interview. I had the distinct feeling that there would be a progression of meetings and an eventual invitation to either volunteer or join the paid staff. My suspicion was confirmed when, as we paid the check for lunch, he mentioned to me that the senior pastor hoped I would take the time to meet with him. I should call and set up an appointment.

I eventually did meet with the pastor. When I asked him why he wanted to see me, he said that he saw the Holy Spirit all over me and he wanted to know my story.

So, I told him. I did not give him as much detail as I am providing here but I identified my partner as my husband. Explained how long we had been together, that we had outlasted most heterosexual marriages and that we intended to marry when gay marriage became legal. As I talked, he deflated and so did my hopes that I had found an open and welcoming congregation. I knew I would be tolerated but not accepted. That we would be kept at a skeptical arm's length.

I suppose I could just attend a church, keep my mouth shut and not open up to anyone. I could attend services, sing songs, listen to the preacher, all the while keeping to myself. But that is not church for me. Church is, or should be, like a family. When I was growing up, our Catholic church was like a family. In the cult, it was like family. In the Bronx, it was like family.

I used to feel guilty for not going to church but my not going to church is a two-way street. I only own half that decision. I do not want to merely attend services wearing a Christian mask, nor do I want to be the defiant one, taking my mask off to confront all the other masks in the pews.

I had hidden behind a mask for so long that I have determined not to do it again and certainly not for the sake of sitting in a church for an hour or two every week. Unless I find a church family that truly accepts me as a child of God and a work in progress, I can live without going to church. I can find my fellowship among people who respect me whether we agree doctrinally or not. This condition seems to be rare in Christendom.

So, we created one.

My husband and I formed a homegroup we called, "Pittsburgh Open-Minded Christians" (POMC). It was at a time when some groups of Christians were forming "organic churches." I was not really interested in forming a church but rather creating a kind of open-minded refuge where people could take off their masks for a little while, at least.

My best friend, who is also a Catholic Deacon, asked me if I intended to draft a statement of faith for the group. He suggested I choose something general like the Apostles Creed.

"That would leave out the Jehovah's Witnesses, the Seventh Day Adventists and the Mormons," was my automatic response. I may not have agreed with some of their doctrines, but I was and remain convinced that one finds sincere believers everywhere. Instead of a statement of faith, I drafted a simple sentence that acknowledged our differences while promoting our unity. *We believe that the teachings and life example of Jesus of Nazareth are worth learning and emulating.*

135

We announced the meeting on social media and got immediate attention. The group met regularly for several years. In that group we had people who came from Fundamentalist, Pentecostal Evangelical, and mainline line Christian denominations, including Methodist, Presbyterian, Lutheran, Roman Catholic, Orthodox, Baptist and Coptic. There were Jehovah's Witnesses, Mormons, Adventists, Gnostics and even one Jewish person.

The meetings were called "Simple Supper." We would usually gather at my home, but several others opened up their homes occasionally. We would share a simple, pot-luck meal while we caught up with one another and made first timers feel welcome. After dinner, we would retire to the living room, with coffee and dessert.

One of us would read a scripture and then we would open up the conversation. There was only one rule. We should not demean or criticize the statement or interpretation of another. All exchanges were to be respectful since we all came from varied backgrounds and were likely to disagree. More than once, I pointed out that disagreement should be illuminating rather than divisive.

Another pastor who attended occasionally found my ability to remain quiet and to not correct doctrine mind boggling. "Correct doctrine is not the point, I said. Notice that these people, nearly every one of them has been injured or damaged in some way by their religion. It is true of me and it is true of you. Correcting their doctrine is not my job and is not appropriate at Simple Supper. We are fostering a healed personal relationship with God; however, they experience it. We want to cultivate a level of comfort in being themselves in a religious context. This is what Simple Supper is all about."

The group turned out to be about fifty percent LGBTQ. Despite the fact that literally half the room was gay, one member attended for over a year before she admitted her same-sex attraction illustrating the degree to which deep-seated religious shame is ingrained.

The first time we shared communion in the group, another member cried. It was the first time in years that she had allowed herself communion because her church rules forbade her from participating in communion because she had been divorced and remarried.

Another member, a disfellowshipped Jehovah's Witness, in the middle of a discussion, raised her head from her Bible and looking straight at me asked, "Does this mean that God is not disgusted with me?" I do not remember the scripture, but I will never forget the look on her face.

Several graduate students in psychology and sociology asked to visit us. Of course, they were permitted to do so; anyone was welcome as long as they followed the rule of respect. A graduate psychology program at an area university would invite me to speak to the students in their graduate counseling program every year for four or five years.

Because of my role as facilitator, many of the attendees came to counsel with me as a pastor. Things they would not share in the group came out then. Some had been sexually abused by a clergy member or family member prominent in the church. They had tales of sitting before judiciary committees, being assigned penitential duties, physical abuse, being excommunicated by church leaders and then shunned by church members. Several had been disowned by their families because of their sexuality. Most, if not all of the attendees felt they could not completely be themselves in any other religious context.

I did not mind running and hosting the meetings but my home, a second-floor walk-up, was not accessible to everyone who wanted to attend. One man who had no legs climbed the twenty-six steps on his hands. Another potential attendee lambasted me because I could not accommodate her wheelchair. I apologized sincerely and offered to schedule at least one meeting in her home. She hung up on me. I tried to find a different location but could not afford the option of renting a space.

We held regular meetings for several years. I had hoped that the group would form a kind of community of mutual support, love, and acceptance. Several friendships among attendees developed but meetings would not occur without me. I prayerfully ended the group fearing it was becoming too centered on me. Anytime a group focuses its attention on a single person, it opens itself up for abuse. I did not and do not think I would have abused the position, but I did not want these people to find themselves in a group like that again.

The time for Simple Supper and Pittsburgh Open-Minded Christians came to an end. Nothing lasts forever.

Chapter 15

It Takes a Miracle

One of the first people I met when starting up POMC was an Evangelical Lutheran pastor. Much to our surprise, we had shared a high school and a band section for a year. I joined the high school marching band in my sophomore year playing tenor sax. She played alto and was a senior. I had admired her talent and skill. My saxophone playing was only strategic for the band. I had played clarinet and the band director asked me to fill in on tenor sax.

We met at a coffee shop, and when we realized that we had casually known one another in youth, we connected easily. She later invited me to her Evangelical Lutheran Pericope meeting, where I acquired the moniker of *Pentecostal Joe*. Every Wednesday, a group of Evangelical Lutheran ministers would meet at a coffee shop to discuss the scriptures that were scheduled for preaching the following Sunday. The Evangelical Lutheran denomination is one of the many that uses a schedule of scripture called a lectionary. The schedule follows a liturgical calendar, and it takes about three years to get through the Bible.

When I was introduced to the group, my background as a Pentecostal minister was presented, and, much to my surprise, I was welcomed into the group.

After some initial social banter, a discussion of the scriptures ensued. These clergy members were highly trained theologically. I greatly benefited from their experience and understanding. The caliber of the conversation climbed several degrees above that which might normally be presented in a sermon. I confess to jotting down notes and looking up references they made.

Often, I imagine out of curiosity, I would be asked what the Pentecostal position or interpretation of certain scriptures or aspects of our discussion might be. I made sure they understood that I could not speak for all Pentecostals as we are not a homogenous group. They would listen intently, perhaps asking further questions or commenting in some way. My opinions or positions were never discounted, and I always felt welcome and validated, even on those rare occasions when we disagreed. It felt good when one or another of them would tell me that my theology was *Lutheran*. I was never sure exactly what that meant beyond we tended to agree on those points. I attended those meetings regularly for well over a year.

One day, I got a call from one of those pastors who now works as a hospital chaplain. Knowing my Pentecostal background, she wanted information about how best to help a Pentecostal family cope with the imminent death of a beloved mother and the probable religious trauma members of the family might suffer.

The woman had experienced some incident or condition that left her without oxygen for a length of time. In that time, she had lost virtually all brain function, including the autonomic functions of the brain that keep one alive such as breathing.

The doctors had made a valiant effort to revive her and to give her every chance of survival. Despite all the medical knowledge applied to save her life, for all intents and purposes, the woman was already dead.

The family was refusing to remove life support, ". . . in order to give God every opportunity to heal her." Her physical body would be moved to a long-term, life support nursing facility where she would have mechanical assistance to breathe and would be fed through a tube quite possibly for many years to come.

The chaplain, though wishing better for the patient, wanted to know how best to minister to the needs of the family, who were likely to be dealt a crisis of faith if and when God did not heal their mother.

Despite their expression of faith, I confess, I doubted the family would be constantly at their mother's side in that facility waiting for the miracle to occur, especially if the miracle were a long time in coming. I also wondered how much opportunity God actually needed to heal the woman and what the family imagined was His reason for waiting. I wondered further how many members of the family considered this episode in their lives a test of their faith.

Many mainstream clergy do not really comprehend the broad range of doctrines held by Pentecostal people. Pentecostals share mostly an experience. Pentecostals believe that what happened on the day of Pentecost should be the experience of most, if not all, true Christians. The kindest expression held about people who do not share their experience is that those Christians are missing out on something wonderful. The most intolerant expression toward people who do not share their experience, is that people who call themselves Christians without evidence of the Baptism in the Holy Spirit is that they are not truly Christian.

There are large denominations associated with Pentecostal expression. The Assembly of God is perhaps the biggest one. Foursquare is another. The aforementioned Sovereign Grace Ministries, though now rebranded as Sovereign Grace Churches, is now an international association of congregations. These share a rather standardized set of doctrines, but many Pentecostal churches are not associated with or perhaps are loosely associated with a larger organization and lack the same kind of accountability structure offered by a denomination.

I have seen what I consider to be miracles. I have already mentioned that I once considered my instantaneous smoking cessation as a miracle. For many years, I did not even entertain the ponderance of why some Christians still smoked or why God did not deliver them of the addiction the way He had delivered me. It was only after years of honest self-examination that I eventually came to understand that my quitting at that moment was really a function of my own emotion and my desire to achieve the goal of total commitment to God rather than a sovereign act of healing or deliverance on His part. It may have not been an actual miracle in the technical sense, but it was a miracle to me.

I have also witnessed cases of spontaneous remission which look, sound, and feel like miracles. Whether we attribute them to a sovereign act of God, thus creating the conundrum of why God does something for some people but not others, or we consider it a miracle that has grown out of the elegant design of being human is inconsequential. Remission is remission.

When I was still an undergraduate a presumed spiritual healer came to speak at our campus fellowship. He asserted that many people, without realizing it, had one leg shorter than the other. We all watched in amazement as he compared the length of the legs of some of our fellows apparently demonstrating that one leg was indeed shorter than the other. For each one, we prayed fervently for God to heal them and to our amazement, we watched the legs come into alignment, the heels coming together to match one another.

It was a parlor trick worked by the angle at which our "healer" held the legs. As for the idea that many people have one leg shorter than the other, it is rarely a deformity in the length of the bones. If it exists at all, the condition is most often otherwise explained. We all favor one leg over the other. As a result, we may slightly tilt our pelvis. It is hardly noticeable but testable.

I recall as a kid, how at a scout meeting in the basement of our church, our scoutmaster challenged us to close our eyes and walk a straight line following the pattern in the linoleum tiles. All of us strayed significantly to one side or the other while thinking we had walked a straight line. The favoring of one leg over the other is indeed ubiquitous, but the miracle is in improving one's posture and musculature, not in God causing bones to grow in an instant.

One evening back in the Bronx, I was visiting another congregation and as usual, there was an invitation to come forward for prayer. Those who were choosing to give their lives to God that evening were directed to one side of the church. All other prayer requests were directed to the other side.

The pastor, a friend of mine had asked me to fill in for an assistant pastor who had been called into work unexpectedly. There were always more prayer requests than new converts, but but I was unfamiliar with the church's process for working with them.. I would be joining a deacon and deaconess from his congregation in praying for the sick or for other prayer requests.

A couple came forward for prayer and went to our line. The woman was visibly pregnant. She walked slowly and with some apparent discomfort, her hand cradling her belly.

"We're going into the hospital in the morning. They are having trouble finding a heartbeat," the husband confided.

I was all set to pray for God's grace over the entire situation, to bless the skills of the doctors and nurses, and for comfort for the couple as they went through this process. In the middle of my prayer, the deaconess, began loudly speaking in tongues and raised her voice above my own. The deacon was inspired to interpret the tongues. The baby was fine. He would grow up to be a great man of God and an amazing evangelist.

Generally, the speaking in and interpretation of tongues are innocuous and for the most part harmless. When this occurs, it is usually a broad exhortation to stay strong in faith and endure whatever trials might be at hand. However, this one was too specific and, I admit now, I had a bad feeling about it. I said nothing to the couple mostly because they were completely caught up in the event. I did not want to be the one seeding doubt and it was not my church.

After we had prayed for everyone, I pulled the pastor aside, told him about the couple going to the hospital in the morning. I also told him about the tongues and the interpretation. I just wanted him to be prepared.

He called me the next day from the hospital. The baby was dead. Not only did the couple have to face the loss of a child, they suffered the additional trauma of what to them seemed to be a failed promise of God.

I know miracles happen. I just do not know how many of our miracles are just things that we do not yet understand. There are seemingly inexplicable spontaneous healings or circumstances seem to just fall into place when they might have gone terribly wrong. I considered the offer of a position in Japan a miracle of provision when Kuwait seemed to be falling through. It is one thing to believe that God works miracles. It is another to assume or demand that he performs the miracle we most want or choose.

God is not intimidated by science. If God is God, He created science. Some people choose to see scientific explanation as an argument against the existence of God. Some Christians actually reject science because of that notion, but the sentiment is not logical. Scientific explanations are factual. Why should God be intimidated by facts?

The loss of that baby was a sobering event in my life as well. I hope it was a sobering even in the lives of those church deacons. The event played a critical role in another demand for a miracle that presented itself much later.

One day, I was visiting with one of families of the church in the Bronx. As we often did, we prayed together. A recent examination of the wife, and mother of two rambunctious boys, discovered a number of possible irregularities on her ovaries. The doctors wanted to do a biopsy. She preferred to believe God for a miracle of healing rather than go through the surgery.

The demand for a miracle gnawed at me for days. I felt her faith came out of a fear of the surgery more than firm conviction. As a pastor, I decided to act. The following Sunday at church, I pulled the husband aside and asked him how he intended to raise his children alone. He was taken aback. I imagine he thought I was prophesying. At least I had is full attention.

"Look," I said. "If you and your wife want to believe for a healing miracle, let the doctors provide the verification of it. As it stands, your wife has spots on her ovaries. They may not be significant, on the other hand, they may be extremely significant. We should not attempt to force the hand of God because we happen to be afraid of surgery. If she ignores the God-given knowledge and training of her doctors by not having a simple biopsy, and those spots are cancerous, you may well be raising your children alone. The spots may be nothing and, if they are nothing, your family will be better off knowing that."

I have no idea which course they eventually took. They chose not to confide in me after that. If she opted out of the surgery and nothing happened, was it a miracle or were those spots on her ovaries simply benign? If she went ahead with the biopsy and discovered the spots were benign, was it a miracle or just benign spots? If she went ahead with the biopsy, discovered early-stage cancer, went through treatment, and went into complete remission, how is that any less of a miracle?

I am willing to hope, pray and even believe for a miracle but I am not going to limit the way the miracle happens. I do not have to believe in magic or fairytales to be faithful. Miracles do not have to be supernatural to be miracles.

When I was a child, I had a book called *Stone Soup*. I believe the story is a European folktale that has a fairly clear moral behind it. I will tell a condensed version of the story in my own words.

One day, three soldiers were walking home from the battle. They were tired and hungry, but happy to finally be going home. In the distance, they saw a tiny village along the road. One soldier spoke up. "Perhaps they will be kind and feed us." Another said, "Unlikely. The war has been difficult for everyone. Perhaps they are as hungry as we are." The third remained silent.

The war had been exceedingly difficult on the people of the village, and more than once their food stores had been commandeered by soldiers. When they saw these soldiers coming down the road, one of them said, "We don't have enough for ourselves, let alone feed these soldiers. They will take everything for themselves, and we will have nothing." Everyone quickly hid every scrap of food, every crust of bread.

When the soldiers arrived in the village, they asked the villagers if they would please give them something to eat.

"So very sorry, good soldiers," they said. "The war has been terrible for our village. We are starving, and harvest is long away."

The third soldier, normally a quiet young man, spoke. "We see. Perhaps we can just rest here for the night." The villages glanced at one another. How could they refuse such a simple expression of hospitality? "Perhaps we could build a fire to keep warm. We won't be any trouble at all."

The villagers agreed and helped them build a fire. As they did so, the third soldier spoke again. "See here. Some of these stones lining this path are soup stones. None of us will starve." He picked up several of the stones and held them out for inspection. "We can make stone soup. If someone has a big pot, we can put it on the fire."

The villagers, of course, were very curious. No one had ever heard of stone soup. Soup from stones . . . it sounded like a miracle. One of the villagers produced a large cooking pot. Together they filled the pot with water from the well and put it on the fire. The soldier dropped the soup stones into the pot. "Now all we have to do is wait."

As they all sat companionably around the fire, waiting for the pot to boil, the third soldier, one who had rarely ever spoken said softly to himself but loud enough for a villager to hear, "If we only had an onion, that would make this soup perfect." The curiosity of the villagers grew. Everyone wanted to know the recipe for stone soup. The villager said, "You know, I think I may know where to find an onion. Let me go and see."

In a few moments, he produced an onion. They put it into the pot.

As the pot began heating up, the aroma of the onion was enticing. "If we only had a few potatoes," one of the soldiers said, catching on to what the third soldier was doing. "In my village, we put in a few potatoes. It's like heaven."

Sure enough, someone in the village produced a few potatoes, and into the pot they went. As time passed, ingredient by ingredient, the villages took from their meager stores, and soon they had a pot of soup big enough to feed the entire village and the soldiers too.

Of course, the moral of the story is about cooperation, sharing resources and valuing community. How many times in life have we seen people pull together and do extraordinary things when confronting a disaster?

Now let me tell you another story.

One day, many people came out to a remote field to hear a powerful preacher. The preacher, sensing the late hour and the hunger of the crowd, told his helpers to feed them. "Impossible," they exclaimed. We do not have enough money to buy food for all these people.

Hearing the dilemma, one young boy offered his small lunch to help out. The helpers rolled their eyes, but the preacher thanked the young man, took his lunch, and gave thanks to God for the food. When he was done praying, he gave the food to his helpers to distribute to the crowd. Everyone ate to their full satisfaction and after the meal, basketfuls of leftovers were collected.

How do you read this story? Did the boy's lunch miraculously grow and multiply as it was passed from person to person or did the gesture cause everyone to share their own lunches with one another only to realize they had an abundance? Which would be the greater miracle?

As for the family coping with the imminent loss of their mother, which would be a greater expression of their faith? Which would be a better miracle? Should they keep her body alive waiting for God to be ready to do something supernatural or should they love and appreciate the grace of having had such a wonderful mother in their lives while letting her go peacefully off to her rest and believing God for comfort in their loss?

Chapter 16

True Worship

Something truly puzzles me. What does God get out of worship? Early in my life, worship was about self-sacrifice, attending church, singing hymns, participating in the mass, going to confession, taking communion, lighting candles, and putting money in the collection plate. All were a kind of offering to God. In my adult Pentecostal life, not much had changed except instead of kneeling in church, we danced, spoke in tongues, sang in the spirit, held our hands up and told God how wonderful he was.

To some degree, all of these acts are self-serving. They make us feel better. They keep us focused. They are by nature, uplifting activities. An attitude of worship may and should underlay all these behaviors. Even a brief reading of 1 Corinthians 13 tells us that acts of worship in and of themselves are meaningless and may well be offensive if they are not borne of love.

It has also been my impression that for some, at least, the behaviors are a kind of extorted compliance. They are done, not out of an attitude to worship but out of a mindset of submission. This is what good Christians do, and failing to do these things marks us in a negative way.

As an adult, I have rarely felt that way because, Pentecostal worship is quite fun. If something were bothering or hindering my participation, I would just sit down, pray, and respectfully wait. But I am certain that some people must be just going through the motions.

For five years of my working life, I worked for an organization that counseled people who found themselves in a financial crisis. I was the Director of Education for Consumer Credit Counseling Service of Los Angeles. In those years, I encountered many Christians who would feed their children the cheapest, junkiest food in order to keep up their tithe. They had huge credit card debt, made minimum payments, and fed their children garbage to keep their pastor in a new car every year. They believed that God would not bless them if they failed to drop their ten percent into the basket.

In advising them on their finances, I would never contradict their religious expression. I often encouraged them to confide in their pastor about alternative ways of making their tithe commitment, perhaps by doing some work around the church or volunteering in some way. I am thankful none of them ever came back to me saying their pastor demanded only cold, hard cash.

I wonder where that idea came from? Do you suppose that God needs their tithe in order to continue His ministry? Do you think He wants children to consume cheap, processed foods instead of healthy delicious food so the pastor can eat meat and veggies all week long? When did the kingdom of God become an extortion racket worthy of the mob?

In the decades since my journey in the desert, my worship has taken on a quite different tone. I no longer raise my hands or dance around a church in excitement. I speak in tongues only privately, and only when I really do not know how to pray. I do not consider doing so as much worship as I do my own limited human perspective for my own comfort and assurance. I do sometimes sing hymns or songs of praise, including Child of Destiny, but I have to admit, I enjoy that. I like singing and I sing pretty well when I am on my own and no one is listening except God and our pet cat, Abbey.

Let me take you for a moment back to my last sermon before leaving New York. You will remember that if someone says he loves God but hates his brother, he is a liar. And, we are to love our neighbors as we love ourselves. I have learned to love myself and have acquired the ability to extend that love to my fellow human beings, even those whom, in my human frailty, I do not particularly like. It is not always easy, but I am working on it.

In fact, the only way I have of worshiping God or serving God is to love and serve His children. All of them, not just the ones who call themselves Christians. My husband and I do go to church sometimes and if I ever find one where I do not have to wear a mask, we might both attend regularly. He is open to it and so am I.

I confess my sins when inspiration or the Holy Spirit tells me that I have behaved in an unbecoming or inappropriate manner toward another person. Hurting another person is, in my opinion, the antithesis of worship and is one of the few things I will define as a committed sin. I gave up lists of sins years ago. (Matthew 25:40)

I am not a doormat, but rarely do I need to stand my doctrinal ground. Who am I to convince someone that my doctrine is better or more correct than theirs? When we disagree, it is on a human but fully respectful level. If I am asked what I believe, I can and do answer sometimes. Usually, I do not answer because it is often a snare to trap me into an argument or someone tries to prove why my belief is incorrect.

More than ten percent of my life is offered in acknowledgment of the privilege and blessings I have received. A generous percentage of my professional practice is offered to those who cannot afford my services. I help out physically and financially when I can and when it is appropriate.

These are my true acts of worship. I have no other way and frankly no better way of demonstrating the awe I experience of the divine.

I am certain that a number of people reading this book may be disinclined to worship in any way. That is perfectly natural for some. Religious trauma may cause our emotional mind to want to skip over those activities because acts of worship may trigger memories and feelings we understandably prefer to avoid.

In the bible, there is a story of a couple named Ananias and Sapphira who sold a property and pledged all the proceeds to the church. They kept some of the money for themselves and when confronted with their deception, they dropped dead (Acts 5:1-11). A careful reading of this passage, no matter which translation you choose, should reveal a manipulative story designed to strike fear in congregants. If this event actually happened at all, Ananias and Sapphira dropped dead of their fear, not the judgment of God. If it had been the judgment of God, lots of pastors, including those that take food from the mouths of poor children to feather their own nests would be dropping dead. This passage has been used by countless charlatans, false teachers, false prophets, and even well-meaning pastors to extort commitment and money from people.

God has no lack and no need of anyone's worship. Despite seeing through every kind of deception from overt lies to self-delusion, God remains compassionate, loving and accepting. Whether done in a mindset of worship or not, acts that are a true expression of worship do more for us than God and He knows that.

As I have already mentioned, I no longer feel inclined to worship using public displays of emotion or behavior. They are just not how I worship any more. I suppose if I were to find a fully accepting church, one in which I felt welcomed and appreciated, I might choose to worship that way again but for now, I keep it private.

I benefit from private worship in two ways. First, my self-esteem and my sense of stewardship are enhanced knowing that I am an active participant in the communities in which I live and work. I see my participation as having real value. Others may or may not notice but what I do does not depend on applause or even gratitude. I do it because I want to do what I see needs to be done.

Secondly, I am in control of it. There is no sense of debt or obligation. I know it sounds counterintuitive to someone who thinks of worship as some sort of offering or sacrifice. I sometimes do sacrifice things for others but that is because I value the benefit that others receive over the value of what I sacrifice.

Do you remember Teddy, the APLA client who loved Mary Jane candies? Well, I liked them, too. I could have easily eaten the stash I kept in my desk drawer, but I saved them for Teddy because I knew how much he liked them. I wanted to give him that gift and I derived pleasure in giving it. In a small way, I sacrificed my own immediate pleasure to give Teddy the enjoyment of treat. It was no real sacrifice at all.

I might do something like that even on a much larger scale and while the sacrifice might be larger, so is the benefit.

The more you grow in love, first for yourself and then toward others, what I call acts of worship become perfectly natural. I choose to see them as an expression of my spirituality, of my becoming more like Jesus. I suspect that most people would not notice them at all and if they did, they might just think I am a nice guy.

And why should I not be a nice guy? After all, I really do believe that the teachings and life-example of Jesus of Nazareth, as I understand them, and as much as we know of them, are worth learning and emulating.

Chapter 17

The Decision is Yours and Yours Alone

There is a verse in the bible that suggests that God can take any situation and turn it into an instrument of love, benefit, and peace (Romans 8:28). If we are God's children, if God lives in and through us, then we have both the ability and, in some ways, the duty to do the same thing. There was a day at AIDS Project Los Angeles that I understood that everything from the bullying I suffered growing up, to my time as a child of destiny, to my shunning by the cult, to my struggle and ultimate acceptance of my sexuality all combined to make me who I was, the ideal person to be in that position.

I am not at all suggesting that God made those things happen to prepare me, but I can see how those terrible experiences have been redeemed. No matter what we experience, we can use our experiences for the benefit of others. If we do so, in a real sense, we redeem the experience.

After all that I have been through, I genuinely like and respect myself. That last sermon of mine impacted the rest of my life. Perhaps

157

the message was more for me than the congregation. I hope others benefitted in some way.

I had to be able to stop being a victim to become a victor. If you have been a victim, I hope you to will choose to now become a victor. The following are suggestions for your path. I think it is best to work through these steps with an experienced person, a therapist or hypnotist experienced in religious trauma.

Remember always that we are creatures whose memories inform our perceptions and whose perceptions create the belief upon which we act. We must rediscover trust in our perceptions and operate on the belief they create. I am not talking about religious belief. I have made it clear that I am not interested in telling you what you should believe but that belief itself is essential to your safety and survival.

If you have been the victim of any kind of trauma that you relive when you think about it, you still need to process what happened to you. Processing the trauma will make it a thing of the past. Processing will not erase the memory but will create an emotional distance effectively putting the event or events in a healthier perspective. They become just something that happened, but they should not be more than that. If when you think of your experience you become angry or relive the event in your head, if your body reacts to the memory, if you feel like running away or doing something drastic either to things, like destroying something, or to other people, like hurting them, or to yourself, you have not sufficiently processed the trauma to move forward. I can write this book now only because I am no longer in turmoil over what happened to me. I am no longer angry at anyone, especially myself.

There is a part of you that has been attracted to religious concepts. That part of you needs to be recognized, comforted, and nurtured. Often victims of religious trauma abandon any semblance of the eternal or divine in their lives. In doing so, many effectively amputate an important aspect of themselves, something that makes them unique and can empower them in their lives. Certainly, it is possible to live and thrive without religious expression but there is no reason to sacrifice that part of you to the perpetrators of your trauma. When you can once again trust your perceptions, you may find that attraction to something bigger than you are, a purpose that goes beyond a day-to-day routine. I hope you will indulge it, broaden your search, read, ask questions, visit, try but always using your experience to keep you sober-minded about it.

Most importantly, do not be afraid to judge. Judge the answers or lack of them that you receive. Do not join a group because the people are nice. Do not join a religious group because you think they have something you do not. If something you try does not work for you, try something else. Most of all, look for that kernel of belief, that seed of faith, that which you actually do believe. Do not simply determine that you do not believe something because in doing so, you open yourself up to influence. As long as your motivation is merely away-from something and not towards something else, you are directionless. It is alright to be directionless while you convalesce but sooner or later, recovery requires effort and direction. Find out what it is that you do believe and state that belief in a positive sentence. It is better to say, for example, "I believe that the direction for my life is in my hands." Rather than, "I do not believe God has a plan for my life."

If you blame yourself at all, or recriminate yourself for having "been so stupid," stop it and stop it now. You did what you did at the time because you thought it was the best thing to do. It may have been the only thing you were capable of doing at the time. Hindsight reveals possibilities to which we were previously blind. You may think you should have known better but the mere fact that you did not know better is an argument against that point. Given all the circumstances as you understood them, you did the best you could at the time.

While it may feel good to call out those who are to blame for your trauma, be careful of your motivation. They did something bad, perhaps heinously bad. But attacking them as an act of angry revenge has limited use and power. In fact, it drains your power and credibility while barely touching them. Exposing the perpetrators of abuse is useful in that it may protect possible future victims. If this is your true motive, then go for it. But no matter how much you cause the perpetrators to suffer, your vengeance will never be satisfied. Feeding that sense of vengeance is ultimately an act of self-sabotage.

You have every right to be angry, but if you let that anger fester into bitterness, it will consume you. Anger is useful because it can motivate you to make changes that are to your benefit and to the benefit of others. At some point, in order to heal, you will need to let go of the anger, or it will fester into bitterness. You may not be ready to do it now but keep the possibility of letting go in the future at hand. Simply imagine that someday, you will not feel the anger as you do today.

Finally, and this is perhaps the hardest part of our recovery. We have to learn how to forgive. Not forgive in a religious sense but in a "finishing-business" sense. What I mean is this: when we forgive someone, we are not saying that what they did was alright or fixed or even that we have gotten over it. We are actually saying that it was *not alright*. It may *never be fixed* and to some degree *we may never get over it entirely*. But we choose to not carry that baggage with us any longer. We are choosing to no longer hold the marker of debt created by the abuse. We are leaving the perpetrators behind to their fate, and we are not allowing the events to stain the rest of our lives. We are letting go of that burden.

Let go and heal. May you find fulfillment in your life, make your peace with the past, and use your valuable experience, no matter how painful it may have been, for the benefit of anyone who needs it but most of all, you. I wish you well.

About the Author

J oseph Onesta is a board-certified clinical hypnosis practitioner and hypnosis instructor. His certifications include the International Medical and Dental Hypnosis Association (IMDHA), the American Council of Hypnotist Examiners (ACHE) and the International Certification Board of Clinical Hypnotherapy. (ICBCH) where he is also certified as an instructor. He is a frequent featured speaker at hypnosis conferences. Joseph privately mentors and supervises a small number of developing hypnotists. He works regularly with clients who have experienced religious trauma, helping them to achieve a greater sense of peace, understanding and contentment. Though he no longer pastors a church, Joseph Onesta is an ordained interdenominational minister.

He lives with his husband Elihu, and their cat Abby in Pittsburgh, Pennsylvania. When not working or writing, Joseph spends time tending his vegetable garden.

Joseph would love to hear from you if this book has inspired or helped you in any way. He can be reached by email at josephonesta@gmail.com or through his website www.MindPowerPittsburgh.com.

9 781736 187036